ISBN 0-8373-2789-X

C-2789   CAREER EXAMINATION SERIES

This is your
PASSBOOK® for...

Librarian II

SAYVILLE LIBRARY

Test Preparation Study Guide
Questions & Answers

NATIONAL LEARNING CORPORATION

Copyright © 2007 by

National Learning Corporation

212 Michael Drive, Syosset, New York 11791

All rights reserved, including the right of reproduction in whole or in part, in any form or by any means, electronic or mechanical, including photocopying, recording, or by any information storage and retrieval system, without permission in writing from the Publisher.

(516) 921-8888
(800) 645-6337
FAX: (516) 921-8743
www.passbooks.com
sales @ passbooks.com
info @ passbooks.com

PRINTED IN THE UNITED STATES OF AMERICA

PASSBOOK®
NOTICE

This book is *SOLELY* intended for, is sold *ONLY* to, and its use is *RESTRICTED* to *individual*, bona fide applicants or candidates who qualify by virtue of having seriously filed applications for appropriate license, certificate, professional and/or promotional advancement, higher school matriculation, scholarship, or other legitimate requirements of educational and/or governmental authorities.

This book is *NOT* intended for use, class instruction, tutoring, training, duplication, copying, reprinting, excerption, or adaptation, etc., by:

(1) Other Publishers

(2) Proprietors and/or Instructors of "Coaching" and/or Preparatory Courses

(3) Personnel and/or Training Divisions of commercial, industrial, and governmental organizations

(4) Schools, colleges, or universities and/or their departments and staffs, including teachers and other personnel

(5) Testing Agencies or Bureaus

(6) Study groups which seek by the purchase of a single volume to copy and/or duplicate and/or adapt this material for use by the group as a whole without having purchased individual volumes for each of the members of the group

(7) Et al.

Such persons would be in violation of appropriate Federal and State statutes.

PROVISION OF LICENSING AGREEMENTS. — Recognized educational commercial, industrial, and governmental institutions and organizations, and others legitimately engaged in educational pursuits, including training, testing, and measurement activities, may address a request for a licensing agreement to the copyright owners, who will determine whether, and under what conditions, including fees and charges, the materials in this book may be used by them. In other words, a licensing facility *exists* for the legitimate use of the material in this book on other than an individual basis. However, it is asseverated and affirmed here that the materials in this book *CANNOT* be used without the receipt of the express permission of such a licensing agreement from the Publishers.

NATIONAL LEARNING CORPORATION
212 Michael Drive
Syosset, New York 11791

Inquiries re licensing agreements should be addressed to:
  The President
  National Learning Corporation
  212 Michael Drive
  Syosset, New York 11791

PASSBOOK SERIES®

THE *PASSBOOK SERIES®* has been created to prepare applicants and candidates for the ultimate academic battlefield – the examination room.

At some time in our lives, each and every one of us may be required to take an examination – for validation, matriculation, admission, qualification, registration, certification, or licensure.

Based on the assumption that every applicant or candidate has met the basic formal educational standards, has taken the required number of courses, and read the necessary texts, the *PASSBOOK SERIES®* furnishes the one special preparation which may assure passing with confidence, instead of failing with insecurity. Examination questions – together with answers – are furnished as the basic vehicle for study so that the mysteries of the examination and its compounding difficulties may be eliminated or diminished by a sure method.

This book is meant to help you pass your examination provided that you qualify and are serious in your objective.

The entire field is reviewed through the huge store of content information which is succinctly presented through a provocative and challenging approach – the question-and-answer method.

A climate of success is established by furnishing the correct answers at the end of each test.

You soon learn to recognize types of questions, forms of questions, and patterns of questioning. You may even begin to anticipate expected outcomes.

You perceive that many questions are repeated or adapted so that you can gain acute insights, which may enable you to score many sure points.

You learn how to confront new questions, or types of questions, and to attack them confidently and work out the correct answers.

You note objectives and emphases, and recognize pitfalls and dangers, so that you may make positive educational adjustments.

Moreover, you are kept fully informed in relation to new concepts, methods, practices, and directions in the field.

You discover that you are actually taking the examination all the time: you are preparing for the examination by "taking" an examination, not by reading extraneous and/or supererogatory textbooks.

In short, this PASSBOOK®, used directedly, should be an important factor in helping you to pass your test.

LIBRARIAN II

DUTIES

Performs professional library work in technical services, public services, circulation or as head of a small branch. Does original cataloging and classification, performs difficult and involved informational and referral services, compiles bibliographies and assists in the selection of library material. Develops and conducts programs for community groups. May supervise subordinate professional or non-professional staff members. Performs related work as required.

SCOPE OF THE WRITTEN TEST

Written test will cover knowledge, skills, and/or abilities in such areas as:
1. Library Science;
2. Communications and public relations; and
3. Clerical abilities.

HOW TO TAKE A TEST

I. YOU MUST PASS AN EXAMINATION

A. *WHAT EVERY CANDIDATE SHOULD KNOW*

Examination applicants often ask us for help in preparing for the written test. What can I study in advance? What kinds of questions will be asked? How will the test be given? How will the papers be graded?

As an applicant for a civil service examination, you may be wondering about some of these things. Our purpose here is to suggest effective methods of advance study and to describe civil service examinations.

Your chances for success on this examination can be increased if you know how to prepare. Those "pre-examination jitters" can be reduced if you know what to expect. You can even experience an adventure in good citizenship if you know why civil service exams are given.

B. *WHY ARE CIVIL SERVICE EXAMINATIONS GIVEN?*

Civil service examinations are important to you in two ways. As a citizen, you want public jobs filled by employees who know how to do their work. As a job seeker, you want a fair chance to compete for that job on an equal footing with other candidates. The best-known means of accomplishing this two-fold goal is the competitive examination.

Exams are widely publicized throughout the nation. They may be administered for jobs in federal, state, city, municipal, town or village governments or agencies.

Any citizen may apply, with some limitations, such as the age or residence of applicants. Your experience and education may be reviewed to see whether you meet the requirements for the particular examination. When these requirements exist, they are reasonable and applied consistently to all applicants. Thus, a competitive examination may cause you some uneasiness now, but it is your privilege and safeguard.

C. *HOW ARE CIVIL SERVICE EXAMS DEVELOPED?*

Examinations are carefully written by trained technicians who are specialists in the field known as "psychological measurement," in consultation with recognized authorities in the field of work that the test will cover. These experts recommend the subject matter areas or skills to be tested; only those knowledges or skills important to your success on the job are included. The most reliable books and source materials available are used as references. Together, the experts and technicians judge the difficulty level of the questions.

Test technicians know how to phrase questions so that the problem is clearly stated. Their ethics do not permit "trick" or "catch" questions. Questions may have been tried out on sample groups, or subjected to statistical analysis, to determine their usefulness.

Written tests are often used in combination with performance tests, ratings of training and experience, and oral interviews. All of these measures combine to form the best-known means of finding the right person for the right job.

II. HOW TO PASS THE WRITTEN TEST

A. NATURE OF THE EXAMINATION

To prepare intelligently for civil service examinations, you should know how they differ from school examinations you have taken. In school you were assigned certain definite pages to read or subjects to cover. The examination questions were quite detailed and usually emphasized memory. Civil service exams, on the other hand, try to discover your present ability to perform the duties of a position, plus your potentiality to learn these duties. In other words, a civil service exam attempts to predict how successful you will be. Questions cover such a broad area that they cannot be as minute and detailed as school exam questions.

In the public service similar kinds of work, or positions, are grouped together in one "class." This process is known as *position-classification*. All the positions in a class are paid according to the salary range for that class. One class title covers all of these positions, and they are all tested by the same examination.

B. FOUR BASIC STEPS

1) Study the announcement

How, then, can you know what subjects to study? Our best answer is: "Learn as much as possible about the class of positions for which you've applied." The exam will test the knowledge, skills and abilities needed to do the work.

Your most valuable source of information about the position you want is the official exam announcement. This announcement lists the training and experience qualifications. Check these standards and apply only if you come reasonably close to meeting them.

The brief description of the position in the examination announcement offers some clues to the subjects which will be tested. Think about the job itself. Review the duties in your mind. Can you perform them, or are there some in which you are rusty? Fill in the blank spots in your preparation.

Many jurisdictions preview the written test in the exam announcement by including a section called "Knowledge and Abilities Required," "Scope of the Examination," or some similar heading. Here you will find out specifically what fields will be tested.

2) Review your own background

Once you learn in general what the position is all about, and what you need to know to do the work, ask yourself which subjects you already know fairly well and which need improvement. You may wonder whether to concentrate on improving your strong areas or on building some background in your fields of weakness. When the announcement has specified "some knowledge" or "considerable knowledge," or has used adjectives like "beginning principles of..." or "advanced ... methods," you can get a clue as to the number and difficulty of questions to be asked in any given field. More questions, and hence broader coverage, would be included for those subjects which are more important in the work. Now weigh your strengths and weaknesses against the job requirements and prepare accordingly.

3) Determine the level of the position

Another way to tell how intensively you should prepare is to understand the level of the job for which you are applying. Is it the entering level? In other words, is this the position in which beginners in a field of work are hired? Or is it an intermediate or advanced level? Sometimes this is indicated by such words as "Junior" or "Senior" in the class title. Other jurisdictions use Roman numerals to designate the level – Clerk I, Clerk II, for example. The word "Supervisor" sometimes appears in the title. If the level is not indicated by the title, check the description of duties. Will you be working under very close supervision, or will you have responsibility for independent decisions in this work?

4) Choose appropriate study materials

Now that you know the subjects to be examined and the relative amount of each subject to be covered, you can choose suitable study materials. For beginning level jobs, or even advanced ones, if you have a pronounced weakness in some aspect of your training, read a modern, standard textbook in that field. Be sure it is up to date and has general coverage. Such books are normally available at your library, and the librarian will be glad to help you locate one. For entry-level positions, questions of appropriate difficulty are chosen – neither highly advanced questions, nor those too simple. Such questions require careful thought but not advanced training.

If the position for which you are applying is technical or advanced, you will read more advanced, specialized material. If you are already familiar with the basic principles of your field, elementary textbooks would waste your time. Concentrate on advanced textbooks and technical periodicals. Think through the concepts and review difficult problems in your field.

These are all general sources. You can get more ideas on your own initiative, following these leads. For example, training manuals and publications of the government agency which employs workers in your field can be useful, particularly for technical and professional positions. A letter or visit to the government department involved may result in more specific study suggestions, and certainly will provide you with a more definite idea of the exact nature of the position you are seeking.

III. KINDS OF TESTS

Tests are used for purposes other than measuring knowledge and ability to perform specified duties. For some positions, it is equally important to test ability to make adjustments to new situations or to profit from training. In others, basic mental abilities not dependent on information are essential. Questions which test these things may not appear as pertinent to the duties of the position as those which test for knowledge and information. Yet they are often highly important parts of a fair examination. For very general questions, it is almost impossible to help you direct your study efforts. What we can do is to point out some of the more common of these general abilities needed in public service positions and describe some typical questions.

1) General information

Broad, general information has been found useful for predicting job success in some kinds of work. This is tested in a variety of ways, from vocabulary lists to questions about current events. Basic background in some field of work, such as sociology or economics, may be sampled in a group of questions. Often these are principles which have become familiar to most persons through exposure rather than through formal training. It is difficult to advise you how to study for these questions; being alert to the world around you is our best suggestion.

2) Verbal ability

An example of an ability needed in many positions is verbal or language ability. Verbal ability is, in brief, the ability to use and understand words. Vocabulary and grammar tests are typical measures of this ability. Reading comprehension or paragraph interpretation questions are common in many kinds of civil service tests. You are given a paragraph of written material and asked to find its central meaning.

3) Numerical ability

Number skills can be tested by the familiar arithmetic problem, by checking paired lists of numbers to see which are alike and which are different, or by interpreting charts and graphs. In the latter test, a graph may be printed in the test booklet which you are asked to use as the basis for answering questions.

4) Observation

A popular test for law-enforcement positions is the observation test. A picture is shown to you for several minutes, then taken away. Questions about the picture test your ability to observe both details and larger elements.

5) Following directions

In many positions in the public service, the employee must be able to carry out written instructions dependably and accurately. You may be given a chart with several columns, each column listing a variety of information. The questions require you to carry out directions involving the information given in the chart.

6) Skills and aptitudes

Performance tests effectively measure some manual skills and aptitudes. When the skill is one in which you are trained, such as typing or shorthand, you can practice. These tests are often very much like those given in business school or high school courses. For many of the other skills and aptitudes, however, no short-time preparation can be made. Skills and abilities natural to you or that you have developed throughout your lifetime are being tested.

Many of the general questions just described provide all the data needed to answer the questions and ask you to use your reasoning ability to find the answers. Your best preparation for these tests, as well as for tests of facts and ideas, is to be at your physical and mental best. You, no doubt, have your own methods of getting into an exam-taking mood and keeping "in shape." The next section lists some ideas on this subject.

IV. KINDS OF QUESTIONS

Only rarely is the "essay" question, which you answer in narrative form, used in civil service tests. Civil service tests are usually of the short-answer type. Full instructions for answering these questions will be given to you at the examination. But in case this is your first experience with short-answer questions and separate answer sheets, here is what you need to know:

1) Multiple-choice Questions

Most popular of the short-answer questions is the "multiple choice" or "best answer" question. It can be used, for example, to test for factual knowledge, ability to solve problems or judgment in meeting situations found at work.

A multiple-choice question is normally one of three types—
- It can begin with an incomplete statement followed by several possible endings. You are to find the one ending which *best* completes the statement, although some of the others may not be entirely wrong.
- It can also be a complete statement in the form of a question which is answered by choosing one of the statements listed.
- It can be in the form of a problem – again you select the best answer.

Here is an example of a multiple-choice question with a discussion which should give you some clues as to the method for choosing the right answer:

When an employee has a complaint about his assignment, the action which will *best* help him overcome his difficulty is to
    A. discuss his difficulty with his coworkers
    B. take the problem to the head of the organization
    C. take the problem to the person who gave him the assignment
    D. say nothing to anyone about his complaint

In answering this question, you should study each of the choices to find which is best. Consider choice "A" – Certainly an employee may discuss his complaint with fellow employees, but no change or improvement can result, and the complaint remains unresolved. Choice "B" is a poor choice since the head of the organization probably does not know what assignment you have been given, and taking your problem to him is known as "going over the head" of the supervisor. The supervisor, or person who made the assignment, is the person who can clarify it or correct any injustice. Choice "C" is, therefore, correct. To say nothing, as in choice "D," is unwise. Supervisors have and interest in knowing the problems employees are facing, and the employee is seeking a solution to his problem.

2) True/False Questions

The "true/false" or "right/wrong" form of question is sometimes used. Here a complete statement is given. Your job is to decide whether the statement is right or wrong.

SAMPLE: A person-to-person long-distance telephone call costs less than a station-to-station call to the same city.

This statement is wrong, or false, since person-to-person calls are more expensive.

This is not a complete list of all possible question forms, although most of the others are variations of these common types. You will always get complete directions for answering questions. Be sure you understand *how* to mark your answers – ask questions until you do.

V. RECORDING YOUR ANSWERS

For an examination with very few applicants, you may be told to record your answers in the test booklet itself. Separate answer sheets are much more common. If this separate answer sheet is to be scored by machine – and this is often the case – it is highly important that you mark your answers correctly in order to get credit.

An electric scoring machine is often used in civil service offices because of the speed with which papers can be scored. Machine-scored answer sheets must be marked with a pencil, which will be given to you. This pencil has a high graphite content which responds to the electric scoring machine. As a matter of fact, stray dots may register as answers, so do not let your pencil rest on the answer sheet while you are pondering the correct answer. Also, if your pencil lead breaks or is otherwise defective, ask for another.

Since the answer sheet will be dropped in a slot in the scoring machine, be careful not to bend the corners or get the paper crumpled.

The answer sheet normally has five vertical columns of numbers, with 30 numbers to a column. These numbers correspond to the question numbers in your test booklet. After each number, going across the page are four or five pairs of dotted lines. These short dotted lines have small letters or numbers above them. The first two pairs may also have a "T" or "F" above the letters. This indicates that the first two pairs only are to be used if the questions are of the true-false type. If the questions are multiple choice, disregard the "T" and "F" and pay attention only to the small letters or numbers.

Answer your questions in the manner of the sample that follows:

32. The largest city in the United States is
    A. Washington, D.C.
    B. New York City
    C. Chicago
    D. Detroit
    E. San Francisco

1) Choose the answer you think is best. (New York City is the largest, so "B" is correct.)
2) Find the row of dotted lines numbered the same as the question you are answering. (Find row number 32)
3) Find the pair of dotted lines corresponding to the answer. (Find the pair of lines under the mark "B.")
4) Make a solid black mark between the dotted lines.

VI. BEFORE THE TEST

Common sense will help you find procedures to follow to get ready for an examination. Too many of us, however, overlook these sensible measures. Indeed, nervousness and fatigue have been found to be the most serious reasons why applicants fail to do their best on civil service tests. Here is a list of reminders:

- Begin your preparation early – Don't wait until the last minute to go scurrying around for books and materials or to find out what the position is all about.
- Prepare continuously – An hour a night for a week is better than an all-night cram session. This has been definitely established. What is more, a night a

week for a month will return better dividends than crowding your study into a shorter period of time.
- Locate the place of the exam – You have been sent a notice telling you when and where to report for the examination. If the location is in a different town or otherwise unfamiliar to you, it would be well to inquire the best route and learn something about the building.
- Relax the night before the test – Allow your mind to rest. Do not study at all that night. Plan some mild recreation or diversion; then go to bed early and get a good night's sleep.
- Get up early enough to make a leisurely trip to the place for the test – This way unforeseen events, traffic snarls, unfamiliar buildings, etc. will not upset you.
- Dress comfortably – A written test is not a fashion show. You will be known by number and not by name, so wear something comfortable.
- Leave excess paraphernalia at home – Shopping bags and odd bundles will get in your way. You need bring only the items mentioned in the official notice you received; usually everything you need is provided. Do not bring reference books to the exam. They will only confuse those last minutes and be taken away from you when in the test room.
- Arrive somewhat ahead of time – If because of transportation schedules you must get there very early, bring a newspaper or magazine to take your mind off yourself while waiting.
- Locate the examination room – When you have found the proper room, you will be directed to the seat or part of the room where you will sit. Sometimes you are given a sheet of instructions to read while you are waiting. Do not fill out any forms until you are told to do so; just read them and be prepared.
- Relax and prepare to listen to the instructions
- If you have any physical problem that may keep you from doing your best, be sure to tell the test administrator. If you are sick or in poor health, you really cannot do your best on the exam. You can come back and take the test some other time.

VII. AT THE TEST

The day of the test is here and you have the test booklet in your hand. The temptation to get going is very strong. Caution! There is more to success than knowing the right answers. You must know how to identify your papers and understand variations in the type of short-answer question used in this particular examination. Follow these suggestions for maximum results from your efforts:

1) Cooperate with the monitor
The test administrator has a duty to create a situation in which you can be as much at ease as possible. He will give instructions, tell you when to begin, check to see that you are marking your answer sheet correctly, and so on. He is not there to guard you, although he will see that your competitors do not take unfair advantage. He wants to help you do your best.

2) Listen to all instructions
Don't jump the gun! Wait until you understand all directions. In most civil service tests you get more time than you need to answer the questions. So don't be in a hurry.

Read each word of instructions until you clearly understand the meaning. Study the examples, listen to all announcements and follow directions. Ask questions if you do not understand what to do.

3) Identify your papers
Civil service exams are usually identified by number only. You will be assigned a number; you must not put your name on your test papers. Be sure to copy your number correctly. Since more than one exam may be given, copy your exact examination title.

4) Plan your time
Unless you are told that a test is a "speed" or "rate of work" test, speed itself is usually not important. Time enough to answer all the questions will be provided, but this does not mean that you have all day. An overall time limit has been set. Divide the total time (in minutes) by the number of questions to determine the approximate time you have for each question.

5) Do not linger over difficult questions
If you come across a difficult question, mark it with a paper clip (useful to have along) and come back to it when you have been through the booklet. One caution if you do this – be sure to skip a number on your answer sheet as well. Check often to be sure that you have not lost your place and that you are marking in the row numbered the same as the question you are answering.

6) Read the questions
Be sure you know what the question asks! Many capable people are unsuccessful because they failed to *read* the questions correctly.

7) Answer all questions
Unless you have been instructed that a penalty will be deducted for incorrect answers, it is better to guess than to omit a question.

8) Speed tests
It is often better NOT to guess on speed tests. It has been found that on timed tests people are tempted to spend the last few seconds before time is called in marking answers at random – without even reading them – in the hope of picking up a few extra points. To discourage this practice, the instructions may warn you that your score will be "corrected" for guessing. That is, a penalty will be applied. The incorrect answers will be deducted from the correct ones, or some other penalty formula will be used.

9) Review your answers
If you finish before time is called, go back to the questions you guessed or omitted to give them further thought. Review other answers if you have time.

10) Return your test materials
If you are ready to leave before others have finished or time is called, take ALL your materials to the monitor and leave quietly. Never take any test material with you. The monitor can discover whose papers are not complete, and taking a test booklet may be grounds for disqualification.

VIII. EXAMINATION TECHNIQUES

1) Read the general instructions carefully. These are usually printed on the first page of the exam booklet. As a rule, these instructions refer to the timing of the examination; the fact that you should not start work until the signal and must stop work at a signal, etc. If there are any *special* instructions, such as a choice of questions to be answered, make sure that you note this instruction carefully.

2) When you are ready to start work on the examination, that is as soon as the signal has been given, read the instructions to each question booklet, underline any key words or phrases, such as *least, best, outline, describe* and the like. In this way you will tend to answer as requested rather than discover on reviewing your paper that you *listed without describing*, that you selected the *worst* choice rather than the *best* choice, etc.

3) If the examination is of the objective or multiple-choice type – that is, each question will also give a series of possible answers: A, B, C or D, and you are called upon to select the best answer and write the letter next to that answer on your answer paper – it is advisable to start answering each question in turn. There may be anywhere from 50 to 100 such questions in the three or four hours allotted and you can see how much time would be taken if you read through all the questions before beginning to answer any. Furthermore, if you come across a question or group of questions which you know would be difficult to answer, it would undoubtedly affect your handling of all the other questions.

4) If the examination is of the essay type and contains but a few questions, it is a moot point as to whether you should read all the questions before starting to answer any one. Of course, if you are given a choice – say five out of seven and the like – then it is essential to read all the questions so you can eliminate the two that are most difficult. If, however, you are asked to answer all the questions, there may be danger in trying to answer the easiest one first because you may find that you will spend too much time on it. The best technique is to answer the first question, then proceed to the second, etc.

5) Time your answers. Before the exam begins, write down the time it started, then add the time allowed for the examination and write down the time it must be completed, then divide the time available somewhat as follows:
   - If 3-1/2 hours are allowed, that would be 210 minutes. If you have 80 objective-type questions, that would be an average of 2-1/2 minutes per question. Allow yourself no more than 2 minutes per question, or a total of 160 minutes, which will permit about 50 minutes to review.
   - If for the time allotment of 210 minutes there are 7 essay questions to answer, that would average about 30 minutes a question. Give yourself only 25 minutes per question so that you have about 35 minutes to review.

6) The most important instruction is to *read each question* and make sure you know what is wanted. The second most important instruction is to *time yourself properly* so that you answer every question. The third most

important instruction is to *answer every question*. Guess if you have to but include something for each question. Remember that you will receive no credit for a blank and will probably receive some credit if you write something in answer to an essay question. If you guess a letter – say "B" for a multiple-choice question – you may have guessed right. If you leave a blank as an answer to a multiple-choice question, the examiners may respect your feelings but it will not add a point to your score. Some exams may penalize you for wrong answers, so in such cases *only*, you may not want to guess unless you have some basis for your answer.

7) Suggestions
   a. Objective-type questions
      1. Examine the question booklet for proper sequence of pages and questions
      2. Read all instructions carefully
      3. Skip any question which seems too difficult; return to it after all other questions have been answered
      4. Apportion your time properly; do not spend too much time on any single question or group of questions
      5. Note and underline key words – *all, most, fewest, least, best, worst, same, opposite,* etc.
      6. Pay particular attention to negatives
      7. Note unusual option, e.g., unduly long, short, complex, different or similar in content to the body of the question
      8. Observe the use of "hedging" words – *probably, may, most likely,* etc.
      9. Make sure that your answer is put next to the same number as the question
      10. Do not second-guess unless you have good reason to believe the second answer is definitely more correct
      11. Cross out original answer if you decide another answer is more accurate; do not erase until you are ready to hand your paper in
      12. Answer all questions; guess unless instructed otherwise
      13. Leave time for review

   b. Essay questions
      1. Read each question carefully
      2. Determine exactly what is wanted. Underline key words or phrases.
      3. Decide on outline or paragraph answer
      4. Include many different points and elements unless asked to develop any one or two points or elements
      5. Show impartiality by giving pros and cons unless directed to select one side only
      6. Make and write down any assumptions you find necessary to answer the questions
      7. Watch your English, grammar, punctuation and choice of words
      8. Time your answers; don't crowd material

8) Answering the essay question

Most essay questions can be answered by framing the specific response around several key words or ideas. Here are a few such key words or ideas:

M's: manpower, materials, methods, money, management
P's: purpose, program, policy, plan, procedure, practice, problems, pitfalls, personnel, public relations

   a. Six basic steps in handling problems:
      1. Preliminary plan and background development
      2. Collect information, data and facts
      3. Analyze and interpret information, data and facts
      4. Analyze and develop solutions as well as make recommendations
      5. Prepare report and sell recommendations
      6. Install recommendations and follow up effectiveness

   b. Pitfalls to avoid
      1. *Taking things for granted* – A statement of the situation does not necessarily imply that each of the elements is necessarily true; for example, a complaint may be invalid and biased so that all that can be taken for granted is that a complaint has been registered
      2. *Considering only one side of a situation* – Wherever possible, indicate several alternatives and then point out the reasons you selected the best one
      3. *Failing to indicate follow up* – Whenever your answer indicates action on your part, make certain that you will take proper follow-up action to see how successful your recommendations, procedures or actions turn out to be
      4. *Taking too long in answering any single question* – Remember to time your answers properly

IX. AFTER THE TEST

Scoring procedures differ in detail among civil service jurisdictions although the general principles are the same. Whether the papers are hand-scored or graded by machine we have described, they are nearly always graded by number. That is, the person who marks the paper knows only the number – never the name – of the applicant. Not until all the papers have been graded will they be matched with names. If other tests, such as training and experience or oral interview ratings have been given, scores will be combined. Different parts of the examination usually have different weights. For example, the written test might count 60 percent of the final grade, and a rating of training and experience 40 percent. In many jurisdictions, veterans will have a certain number of points added to their grades.

After the final grade has been determined, the names are placed in grade order and an eligible list is established. There are various methods for resolving ties between those who get the same final grade – probably the most common is to place first the name of the person whose application was received first. Job offers are made from the eligible list in the order the names appear on it. You will be notified of your grade and your rank as soon as all these computations have been made. This will be done as rapidly as possible.

People who are found to meet the requirements in the announcement are called "eligibles." Their names are put on a list of eligible candidates. An eligible's chances of getting a job depend on how high he stands on this list and how fast agencies are filling jobs from the list.

When a job is to be filled from a list of eligibles, the agency asks for the names of people on the list of eligibles for that job. When the civil service commission receives this request, it sends to the agency the names of the three people highest on this list. Or, if the job to be filled has specialized requirements, the office sends the agency the names of the top three persons who meet these requirements from the general list.

The appointing officer makes a choice from among the three people whose names were sent to him. If the selected person accepts the appointment, the names of the others are put back on the list to be considered for future openings.

That is the rule in hiring from all kinds of eligible lists, whether they are for typist, carpenter, chemist, or something else. For every vacancy, the appointing officer has his choice of any one of the top three eligibles on the list. This explains why the person whose name is on top of the list sometimes does not get an appointment when some of the persons lower on the list do. If the appointing officer chooses the second or third eligible, the No. 1 eligible does not get a job at once, but stays on the list until he is appointed or the list is terminated.

X. HOW TO PASS THE INTERVIEW TEST

The examination for which you applied requires an oral interview test. You have already taken the written test and you are now being called for the interview test – the final part of the formal examination.

You may think that it is not possible to prepare for an interview test and that there are no procedures to follow during an interview. Our purpose is to point out some things you can do in advance that will help you and some good rules to follow and pitfalls to avoid while you are being interviewed.

What is an interview supposed to test?

The written examination is designed to test the technical knowledge and competence of the candidate; the oral is designed to evaluate intangible qualities, not readily measured otherwise, and to establish a list showing the relative fitness of each candidate – as measured against his competitors – for the position sought. Scoring is not on the basis of "right" and "wrong," but on a sliding scale of values ranging from "not passable" to "outstanding." As a matter of fact, it is possible to achieve a relatively low score without a single "incorrect" answer because of evident weakness in the qualities being measured.

Occasionally, an examination may consist entirely of an oral test – either an individual or a group oral. In such cases, information is sought concerning the technical knowledges and abilities of the candidate, since there has been no written examination for this purpose. More commonly, however, an oral test is used to supplement a written examination.

Who conducts interviews?

The composition of oral boards varies among different jurisdictions. In nearly all, a representative of the personnel department serves as chairman. One of the members of the board may be a representative of the department in which the candidate would work. In some cases, "outside experts" are used, and, frequently, a businessman or some other representative of the general public is asked to serve. Labor and management or other special groups may be represented. The aim is to secure the services of experts in the appropriate field.

However the board is composed, it is a good idea (and not at all improper or unethical) to ascertain in advance of the interview who the members are and what groups they represent. When you are introduced to them, you will have some idea of their backgrounds and interests, and at least you will not stutter and stammer over their names.

What should be done before the interview?

While knowledge about the board members is useful and takes some of the surprise element out of the interview, there is other preparation which is more substantive. It *is* possible to prepare for an oral interview – in several ways:

1) Keep a copy of your application and review it carefully before the interview

This may be the only document before the oral board, and the starting point of the interview. Know what education and experience you have listed there, and the sequence and dates of all of it. Sometimes the board will ask you to review the highlights of your experience for them; you should not have to hem and haw doing it.

2) Study the class specification and the examination announcement

Usually, the oral board has one or both of these to guide them. The qualities, characteristics or knowledges required by the position sought are stated in these documents. They offer valuable clues as to the nature of the oral interview. For example, if the job involves supervisory responsibilities, the announcement will usually indicate that knowledge of modern supervisory methods and the qualifications of the candidate as a supervisor will be tested. If so, you can expect such questions, frequently in the form of a hypothetical situation which you are expected to solve. NEVER go into an oral without knowledge of the duties and responsibilities of the job you seek.

3) Think through each qualification required

Try to visualize the kind of questions you would ask if you were a board member. How well could you answer them? Try especially to appraise your own knowledge and background in each area, *measured against the job sought*, and identify any areas in which you are weak. Be critical and realistic – do not flatter yourself.

4) Do some general reading in areas in which you feel you may be weak

For example, if the job involves supervision and your past experience has NOT, some general reading in supervisory methods and practices, particularly in the field of human relations, might be useful. Do NOT study agency procedures or detailed manuals. The oral board will be testing your understanding and capacity, not your memory.

5) Get a good night's sleep and watch your general health and mental attitude

You will want a clear head at the interview. Take care of a cold or any other minor ailment, and of course, no hangovers.

What should be done on the day of the interview?

Now comes the day of the interview itself. Give yourself plenty of time to get there. Plan to arrive somewhat ahead of the scheduled time, particularly if your appointment is in the fore part of the day. If a previous candidate fails to appear, the board might be ready for you a bit early. By early afternoon an oral board is almost invariably behind schedule if there are many candidates, and you may have to wait.

Take along a book or magazine to read, or your application to review, but leave any extraneous material in the waiting room when you go in for your interview. In any event, relax and compose yourself.

The matter of dress is important. The board is forming impressions about you – from your experience, your manners, your attitude, and your appearance. Give your personal appearance careful attention. Dress your best, but not your flashiest. Choose conservative, appropriate clothing, and be sure it is immaculate. This is a business interview, and your appearance should indicate that you regard it as such. Besides, being well groomed and properly dressed will help boost your confidence.

Sooner or later, someone will call your name and escort you into the interview room. *This is it.* From here on you are on your own. It is too late for any more preparation. But remember, you asked for this opportunity to prove your fitness, and you are here because your request was granted.

What happens when you go in?

The usual sequence of events will be as follows: The clerk (who is often the board stenographer) will introduce you to the chairman of the oral board, who will introduce you to the other members of the board. Acknowledge the introductions before you sit down. Do not be surprised if you find a microphone facing you or a stenotypist sitting by. Oral interviews are usually recorded in the event of an appeal or other review.

Usually the chairman of the board will open the interview by reviewing the highlights of your education and work experience from your application – primarily for the benefit of the other members of the board, as well as to get the material into the record. Do not interrupt or comment unless there is an error or significant misinterpretation; if that is the case, do not hesitate. But do not quibble about insignificant matters. Also, he will usually ask you some question about your education, experience or your present job – partly to get you to start talking and to establish the interviewing "rapport." He may start the actual questioning, or turn it over to one of the other members. Frequently, each member undertakes the questioning on a particular area, one in which he is perhaps most competent, so you can expect each member to participate in the examination. Because time is limited, you may also expect some rather abrupt switches in the direction the questioning takes, so do not be upset by it. Normally, a board member will not pursue a single line of questioning unless he discovers a particular strength or weakness.

After each member has participated, the chairman will usually ask whether any member has any further questions, then will ask you if you have anything you wish to add. Unless you are expecting this question, it may floor you. Worse, it may start you off on an extended, extemporaneous speech. The board is not usually seeking more information. The question is principally to offer you a last opportunity to present further qualifications or to indicate that you have nothing to add. So, if you feel that a significant qualification or characteristic has been overlooked, it is proper to point it out in a sentence or so. Do not compliment the board on the thoroughness of their examination – they have been sketchy, and you know it. If you wish, merely say, "No thank you, I have nothing further to add." This is a point where you can "talk yourself out" of a good impression or fail to present an important bit of information. Remember, *you close the interview yourself.*

The chairman will then say, "That is all, Mr. _____, thank you." Do not be startled; the interview is over, and quicker than you think. Thank him, gather your belongings and take your leave. Save your sigh of relief for the other side of the door.

How to put your best foot forward

Throughout this entire process, you may feel that the board individually and collectively is trying to pierce your defenses, seek out your hidden weaknesses and embarrass and confuse you. Actually, this is not true. They are obliged to make an appraisal of your qualifications for the job you are seeking, and they want to see you in your best light. Remember, they must interview all candidates and a non-cooperative candidate may become a failure in spite of their best efforts to bring out his qualifications. Here are 15 suggestions that will help you:

1) Be natural – Keep your attitude confident, not cocky

If you are not confident that you can do the job, do not expect the board to be. Do not apologize for your weaknesses, try to bring out your strong points. The board is interested in a positive, not negative, presentation. Cockiness will antagonize any board member and make him wonder if you are covering up a weakness by a false show of strength.

2) Get comfortable, but don't lounge or sprawl

Sit erectly but not stiffly. A careless posture may lead the board to conclude that you are careless in other things, or at least that you are not impressed by the importance of the occasion. Either conclusion is natural, even if incorrect. Do not fuss with your clothing, a pencil or an ashtray. Your hands may occasionally be useful to emphasize a point; do not let them become a point of distraction.

3) Do not wisecrack or make small talk

This is a serious situation, and your attitude should show that you consider it as such. Further, the time of the board is limited – they do not want to waste it, and neither should you.

4) Do not exaggerate your experience or abilities

In the first place, from information in the application or other interviews and sources, the board may know more about you than you think. Secondly, you probably will not get away with it. An experienced board is rather adept at spotting such a situation, so do not take the chance.

5) If you know a board member, do not make a point of it, yet do not hide it

Certainly you are not fooling him, and probably not the other members of the board. Do not try to take advantage of your acquaintanceship – it will probably do you little good.

6) Do not dominate the interview

Let the board do that. They will give you the clues – do not assume that you have to do all the talking. Realize that the board has a number of questions to ask you, and do not try to take up all the interview time by showing off your extensive knowledge of the answer to the first one.

7) Be attentive

You only have 20 minutes or so, and you should keep your attention at its sharpest throughout. When a member is addressing a problem or question to you, give him your undivided attention. Address your reply principally to him, but do not exclude the other board members.

8) Do not interrupt

A board member may be stating a problem for you to analyze. He will ask you a question when the time comes. Let him state the problem, and wait for the question.

9) Make sure you understand the question

Do not try to answer until you are sure what the question is. If it is not clear, restate it in your own words or ask the board member to clarify it for you. However, do not haggle about minor elements.

10) Reply promptly but not hastily

A common entry on oral board rating sheets is "candidate responded readily," or "candidate hesitated in replies." Respond as promptly and quickly as you can, but do not jump to a hasty, ill-considered answer.

11) Do not be peremptory in your answers

A brief answer is proper – but do not fire your answer back. That is a losing game from your point of view. The board member can probably ask questions much faster than you can answer them.

12) Do not try to create the answer you think the board member wants

He is interested in what kind of mind you have and how it works – not in playing games. Furthermore, he can usually spot this practice and will actually grade you down on it.

13) Do not switch sides in your reply merely to agree with a board member

Frequently, a member will take a contrary position merely to draw you out and to see if you are willing and able to defend your point of view. Do not start a debate, yet do not surrender a good position. If a position is worth taking, it is worth defending.

14) Do not be afraid to admit an error in judgment if you are shown to be wrong

The board knows that you are forced to reply without any opportunity for careful consideration. Your answer may be demonstrably wrong. If so, admit it and get on with the interview.

15) Do not dwell at length on your present job

The opening question may relate to your present assignment. Answer the question but do not go into an extended discussion. You are being examined for a *new* job, not your present one. As a matter of fact, try to phrase ALL your answers in terms of the job for which you are being examined.

Basis of Rating

Probably you will forget most of these "do's" and "don'ts" when you walk into the oral interview room. Even remembering them all will not ensure you a passing grade. Perhaps you did not have the qualifications in the first place. But remembering them will help you to put your best foot forward, without treading on the toes of the board members.

Rumor and popular opinion to the contrary notwithstanding, an oral board wants you to make the best appearance possible. They know you are under pressure – but they also want to see how you respond to it as a guide to what your reaction would be under the pressures of the job you seek. They will be influenced by the degree of poise you display, the personal traits you show and the manner in which you respond.

EXAMINATION SECTION

EXAMINATION SECTION
TEST 1

Directions: Each question or incomplete statement is followed by several suggested answers or completions. Select the one that BEST answers the question or completes the statement. *PRINT THE LETTER OF THE CORRECT ANSWER IN THE SPACE AT THE RIGHT.*

1) A library is in the process of conducting an annual performance evaluation. Which of the following would be an output measure that might be used in this process?

A. Staff expenditures
B. User satisfaction survey results
C. Ratio of computer workstations to daily average users
D. Ratio of interlibrary loan lending to borrowing

1. _____

2) The _____ record is a separate record attached to the bibliographic record for a serial title in which the receipt of individual issues or parts is entered on an ongoing basis.

A. holdings
B. check-in
C. item
D. periodical

2. _____

3) Of the following, which research tool would be most appropriate for finding where an author uses specific words or phrases?

A. Abstract
B. Gazetteer
C. Dictionary
D. Concordance

3. _____

4) In library cataloging, a separately published part of a bibliographic resource, usually representing a subject category within the whole and indicated by a topical heading or an alphanumeric heading, is a(n)

A. class
B. scope
C. notch
D. section

4. _____

5) The main advantage to paying an electronic journal publisher on a per-article basis, rather than subscribing to a package or database, is that

A. hardware, browser, and networking requirements are simpler
B. the library pays only for what it uses
C. costs are shifted entirely to the user
D. costs are more predictable over time

5. _____

6) The Dublin Core Metadata Initiative, an international effort to develop standard mechanisms for searching online resources, has named 15 core metadata elements to be used to direct searches. Which of the following is NOT one of these?

A. Editor
B. Rights
C. Date
D. Format

6. _____

7) "Converting" electronic records means that

A. there is a change to the underlying bit stream, but there is no change in the representation or intellectual content of the records
B. they are moved from a proprietary legacy system that lacks software functionality to an open system
C. they have been transferred from old storage media to new storage media with the same format specifications and without any loss in structure, content, or context
D. they have been exported or imported from one software environment to another without the loss of structure, content, or context even though the underlying bit stream has likely been altered

7. _____

8) The 3XX fields in the MARC system contain

A. physical descriptions
B. main entries
C. subject added entries
D. titles, editions, and imprints

8. _____

9) In Internet user, instead of being taken to a desired Web page, instead is taken to a page that says *Error Message 404*. What has happened?

A. Either the server is busy, or the site has moved.
B. Special permission is needed to access the site.
C. The file has been moved or deleted, or the URL in incorrect.
D. The syntax used in the URL is incorrect.

9. _____

10) An anthology is compiled by 6 authors. According to the MLA format, how many of the author's names should be included in a citation?

A. 0
B. 1
C. 2
D. 6

10. _____

11) Which of the following is NOT an advantage of using HTML as a format for file preservation?

A. Extensive authoring tools
B. Improving tools for conversion-to-HTML
C. Good standard for delivering simple text
D. Can be viewed in any browser

11. _____

12) In the MARC record, the same digits are assigned across fields in the second and third character positions of the tag to indicate data of the same type. For example, tags reading "X10" contain information about

A. topical terms
B. bibliographic titles
C. uniform titles
D. corporate names

12. _____

13) A librarian wants to subscribe to an e-mail newsletter that contains annotations of information technology articles and other items written by a team of librarians and library staff. She is wary, however, of having her inbox clogged with unread material that arrives too frequently for her to read it all, and would prefer to have the newsletter arrive monthly. The librarian should subscribe to

A. *Free Pint*
B. *Edupage*
C. *Current Cites*
D. *NewsScan*

13. _____

14) A journal's "impact factor," a measure of its relative importance, is most often defined as the _____ in a given year.

A. number of electronic queries coming from a library database
B. frequency of citations to its articles
C. number of top-rated professionals or scholars who publish in it
D. times the full-text is displayed on a library terminal

14. _____

15) _____ is the online database designed and maintained since 1995 by the Library of Congress to make legislative information accessible to the public

A. CQ
B. NARA
C. THOMAS
D. FindLaw

15. _____

16) The main software protocol that manages data on the Internet is

A. TCP/IP
B. HTTP
C. HTML
D. FTP

16. _____

17) Which of the following is a repeatable MARC field?

A. 100
B. 246
C. 250
D. 260

17. _____

18) A user seeking articles about transportation should be directed to Wilson's _____ Index.

A. Social Sciences
B. Business Periodicals
C. Applied Science and Technology
D. General Science

18. _____

19) In the library literature, materials designated with the collecting level "4" in relation to a given subject are considered

A. "out of scope"
B. sources of basic information
C. comprehensive and authoritative
D. useful for the support of research in the given subject

19. _____

20) In Web addresses, the hashmark is used to

A. create a link to another location in the same document
B. identify a port
C. create a link to another Web page
D. differentiate numerical characters

20. _____

21) The content of a Web site is difficult to navigate, and users tend to get confused when trying to find information. The resource assessment guideline that needs to be addressed is

21. _____

A. Documentation and Credibility
B. Ease of Use, Navigation, and Accessibility
C. User Interface and Design
D. Content

22) To extend the accessibility of any material that can be displayed at a library workstation to those with extremely poor vision, _____ can be used.

22. _____

A. screen reading software
B. screen magnifying software
C. TTY
D. an on-screen keyboard

23) The software application needed to read files in Portable Document Format (PDF) is known as

23. _____

A. Acrobat Reader
B. Real Page
C. Pagemaker
D. techexplorer Hypermedia Browser

24) In data that is prepared in the cataloging-in-publication (CIP) format and distributed in MARC format prior to a work's publication, the element that typically appears after the notes about bibliographical references or previous editions is the

24. _____

A. Library of Congress classification number
B. statement of responsibility
C. ISBN
D. Dewey Decimal classification number

25) The reason for the slow pace of initial acceptance of WORM (write once, read many) technology in library archiving is that

25. _____

A. the amount of storage available on the disks is too variable to offer predictable capacity
B. disks are not standardized and can be read only on the type of drive used to write them
C. the data cannot be altered once it is stored
D. the longevity of the disk media is still unknown

KEY (CORRECT ANSWERS)

1. D
2. B
3. D
4. D
5. B

6. A
7. D
8. A
9. C
10. B

11. A
12. D
13. C
14. B
15. C

16. A
17. B
18. C
19. D
20. A

21. B
22. A
23. A
24. C
25. B

TEST 2

Directions: Each question or incomplete statement is followed by several suggested answers or completions. Select the one that BEST answers the question or completes the statement. *PRINT THE LETTER OF THE CORRECT ANSWER IN THE SPACE AT THE RIGHT.*

1) Which of the following is NOT an aggregator service?

1. _____

A. ScienceDirect
B. JSTOR
C. Britannica
D. Blackwell's Electronic Journal Navigator

2) Technical service librarians are usually concerned with any of the following, EXCEPT

2. _____

A. repairing damaged materials
B. checking in journals
C. cataloging books
D. checking books out

3) Materials that are published electronically are identified by their

3. _____

A. EAD
B. DOI
C. XLS
D. ISBN

4) Which of the following is an example of "mobile code" that allows a Web designer to incorporate computer programs, such as Flash pages, into Web page content?

4. _____

A. Packet
B. Worm
C. Warez
D. Applet

5) The abbreviation "NOP" on a publisher's invoice usually means the requested item

5. _____

A. is on back order
B. is not in print
C. the requested item is not published by the vendor
D. has not yet been published, but will be in the future

6) A well-designed online catalog or bibliographic database allows the user to employ limiting parameters to restrict the retrieval or entries including the terms included in the search statement. Which of the following is NOT a common example of these "limiters?"

6. _____

A. Spelling
B. Publication date
C. Full-text
D. Locally held

7) Which of the following is LEAST likely to be a guideline followed in setting up an electronic reserves (ER) system in an academic library?

7. _____

A. Restrict access to authorized users off-site, but maintain open access on-site.
B. Limit offsite access by course and/or instructor name.
C. Remove or suppress access at the end of every session.
D. Post copyright warning notices.

8) Subsystems of the Internet include

8. _____

   I. the World Wide Web
   II. Newsgroups
   III. Telnet
   IV. e-mail

A. I only
B. I, II and III
C. II and III
D. I, II, III and IV

9) Binary scanning at 300 dot per inch (dpi) is usually considered adequate for

9. _____

A. halftones
B. illustrated text
C. typed or laser-printed archival documents
D. published text/line art

10) The systems librarian's responsibilities typically include each of the following, EXCEPT

10. _____

A. development and maintenance of hardware and software
B. Webmaster
C. training staff in the use of library systems
D. interlibrary loan processing

11) A records survey is LEAST likely to be used for the purpose of determining the _____ of archival records.

A. quality
B. content
C. physical quantities
D. provenance

12) In the searching of an electronic database, which of the following might cause a "false drop?"

A. The omission of older information
B. Too-frequent updating of the database
C. A word with more than one meaning
D. Restrictions on database use

13) A group of librarians is meeting to determine the selection of electronic journals for a library's collection. One of the MOST likely disadvantages of including the reference librarian in this group is that he may not

A. have close contact with users
B. be accustomed to the collaborative approach
C. be able to relinquish his primary responsibilities for long enough periods of time
D. have experience selecting and supporting electronic resources

14) Most Internet service providers (ISPs) are built on _____ lines.

A. 56 Kbps
B. ISDN
C. T-1
D. T-3

15) Which of the following is a term used to denote a hard copy enlargement of an image on microform?

A. Blowback
B. Macroform
C. Aperture card
D. Blowup

16) On the Web or in an online bibliography, well-designed search software is capable of

      I.   searching more than one database simultaneously
      II.   removing duplicate record s from results when searching multiple databases
      III.   viewing search terms highlighted in results
      IV.   printing, e-mailing, and downloading results in various formats

A. I only
B. I and III
C. III only
D. I, II, III and IV

16. _____

17) Subject heading systems do NOT

A. assist searchers in understanding how a specific subject fits into a larger structure of knowledge
B. divide knowledge over 30 broad categories
C. describe what a book or article is about
D. allow people to search by subject area

17. _____

18) In order to ensure the integrity of digital archive, the origin and chain of custody of a particular file or record most be preserved. This feature of information integrity is known as

A. content
B. provenance
C. content
D. fixity

18. _____

19) The creation of a Web page could involve

      I.   using a dedicated Web authoring software program
      II.   converting a word-processed document to HTML
      III.   converting a magazine article, with images, to PDF
      IV.   use the Web authoring capability of a portal

A. I and II
B. I, II and IV
C. II and III
D. II, III and IV

19. _____

20) What is the general term for an indexable concept that is assigned to add depth to subject indexing, and that is not listed in the thesaurus of indexing terms because it either represents a proper name or a concept that is not yet authorized for inclusion in the bibliographic database?

20. _____

A. assigner
B. identifier
C. descriptor
D. ideogram

21) The *World of Learning* is an example of a(n)

21. _____

A. concordance
B. encyclopedia
C. abstract
D. directory

22) In the United States, the professional association for academic libraries and librarians is the

22. _____

A. Association of College and Research Libraries (ACRL)
B. Association of Specialized and Cooperative Library Agencies (ASCLA)
C. American Library Association (ALA)
D. National Commission on Libraries and Information Science (NCLIS)

23) The module of the library automation system that is used by the public for interacting with the system is the

23. _____

A. circulation module
B. serials module
C. OPAC
D. cataloging module

24) Which of the following is a synthetic classification system?

24. _____

A. Dewey Decimal
B. Colon classification
C. Library of Congress classification
D. *Sears List*

25) Library issues concerning the USA Patriot Act include   25. _____

      I.   civil liberties related to privacy and confidentiality
      II.   denial of access to information
      III.   fair use
      IV.   copyright law

A.   I and II
B.   II only
C.   II, III and IV
D.   I, II, III and IV

KEY (CORRECT ANSWERS)

1. C
2. D
3. B
4. D
5. C

6. A
7. A
8. D
9. C
10. D

11. A
12. C
13. C
14. C
15. A

16. D
17. B
18. B
19. B
20. B

21. D
22. A
23. C
24. B
25. A

EXAMINATION SECTION

DIRECTIONS: Each question or incomplete statement is followed by several suggested answers or completions. Select the one that BEST answers the question or completes the statement. *PRINT THE LETTER OF THE CORRECT ANSWER IN THE SPACE AT THE RIGHT.*

1. A book about the life of another person is called a(n) 1.___
   A. monograph   B. fiction   C. biography
   D. autobiography   E. reference

2. A book about real experiences is usually referred to as a(n) 2.___
   A. reference   B. monograph   C. fiction
   D. non-fiction   E. autobiography

3. The Dewey Decimal system is a 3.___
   A. list of books, magazines, and non-print materials
   B. system for checking out books
   C. method for organizing materials on the same subject matter together
   D. system for filing cards
   E. system for networking

4. A catalog card reading MOVIE see MOTION PICTURE means: 4.___
   A. All books on movies will be found under the subject heading MOTION PICTURE
   B. Additional books on movies will be found under the subject heading MOTION PICTURE
   C. Another library has the motion picture holdings
   D. Materials are expected on motion pictures
   E. All materials on movies are circulating

5. A bibliography is a(n) 5.___
   A. encyclopedia   B. networking
   C. means of circulating materials   D. list of materials
   E. reference tool

6. An annotation is a(n) 6.___
   A. review   B. explanatory note   C. precis
   D. format   E. critique

7. AMERICAN REFERENCE BOOKS ANNUAL provides a 7.___
   A. comprehensive reviewing service of reference books published in the United States
   B. monthly periodical furnishing reviews of popular reference tools
   C. publisher's guide to monthly reviewing sources
   D. professional journal published by the American Library Association
   E. bibliography of bibliographies

8. An index is a(n) 8.___
   A. table of contents   B. encyclopedia
   C. series of footnotes   D. bibliography
   E. guide to locate material

9. The library catalog is a(n)
    A. shelf list
    B. index to the materials collection
    C. bibliography
    D. system for reserves
    E. collection of book orders

10. A shelf list is a
    A. record of materials in a library
    B. reserve list
    C. weeding list
    D. list of reference materials
    E. bibliography of reference sources

11. Technical services include
    A. acquisitions, cataloging, and materials preparation
    B. reference work and user services
    C. reader's advisory services
    D. circulation and reference services
    E. networking

12. A collection of materials such as pamphlets, clippings, or illustrations kept in special containers is referred to as a
    A. card catalog   B. card file   C. vertical file
    D. container collection   E. clipping file

13. An electromagnetic recording made for playback on a television set is referred to as a(n)
    A. audio tape   B. cassette   C. video-recording
    D. superdisk   E. fiche

14. A word, name, object, group of words, or acronym describing a subject is usually referred to as a
    A. cross reference   B. subject heading
    C. nom de plume   D. serial   E. catalog card

15. A collection of materials with restricted circulation usually found in college and university libraries is called a(n) _____ collection.
    A. reserved materials   B. patron   C. student
    D. open stack   E. rotating reserve

16. An independent publication of forty-nine pages or less, bound in paper covers, is called a
    A. serial   B. monograph   C. microcard
    D. pamphlet   E. fiche

17. Library work directly concerned with assistance to readers in securing information and in using library resources is termed
    A. circulation services   B. technical services
    C. reader's advisory services   D. user services
    E. networking

18. A three-dimensional representation of a real object reproduced in the original size or to scale is called a(n)
    A. model   B. film   C. microform   D. ultrafiche
    E. videotape

19. The act of filling out required forms to become an eligible   19. ___
    library borrower is called
       A. serialization   B. direction   C. registration
       D. reference work   E. signing

20. A direction in a catalog that guides the user to related   20. ___
    names or subjects is termed a _____ reference.
       A. shelf   B. see-also   C. title   D. see
       E. subject

21. A record of a work in the catalog under the title is called   21. ___
    a A. subject card   B. number entry   C. author card
       D. subject entry   E. title entry

22. The printed scheme of a classification system is referred   22. ___
    to as a
       A. classification schedule   B. numbering schedule
       C. lettering schedule   D. cutter number
       E. copyright

23. The entry of a work in the catalog under the subject head-   23. ___
    ing is called a
       A. subject card   B. subject heading   C. subject entry
       D. reference entry   E. subject guide

24. The department in a library responsible for officially   24. ___
    listing prospective borrowers is the _____ department.
       A. reference   B. registration   C. welcoming
       D. circulation   E. technical

25. Library work that deals with patrons and the use of the   25. ___
    library collection is called _____ services.
       A. technical   B. reader   C. circulation
       D. reference   E. public

26. Material held for a borrower for a limited time is termed   26. ___
    _____ material.
       A. reference   B. reserved   C. circulation
       D. special   E. held

27. A notice sent to a borrower to remind him to return held-   27. ___
    over due material is a(n)
       A. warning   B. notice   C. overdue notice
       D. warning notice   E. call slip

28. Material returned to the library before the date due is   28. ___
       A. penalized   B. returned   C. accepted   D. unneeded
       E. subject to examination

29. Real objects, specimens, or artifacts are called   29. ___
       A. toys   B. realia   C. games   D. opaque material
       E. models

30. A film with a series of pictures in sequence which creates   30. ___
    the illusion of motion when projected is classified as a
       A. photogram   B. motion picture   C. videotape
       D. cassette   E. slide

31. Laying books on the shelves in proper order is called
    A. placing B. weeding C. reading D. shifting E. shelving

32. A publication issued in successive parts usually to be continued indefinitely is referred to as a
    A. paper B. monograph C. serial D. pamphlet E. edition

33. A record of the loan of material is called a
    A. call slip B. reserve C. contract D. copy E. charge

34. Information arranged in tabular, outline, or graphic form on a sheet of paper is called a
    A. classification B. charge C. chart D. catalog E. cartoon

35. The method used to lend materials to borrowers and maintain the necessary records is the _____ system.
    A. classification B. circulation control C. reference
    D. borrowing E. returnable

36. Any entry, other than a subject entry, that is made in a catalog in addition to the main entry is called a(n)
    A. added entry B. call number C. central reference
    D. reference entry E. explanatory entry

37. The record of the number of items charged out of a library is termed
    A. record statistics B. circulation statistics
    C. circulation control D. record control
    E. itemizing

38. A number assigned to each book or item as it is received by the library is referred to as a(n) _____ number.
    A. call B. accession C. entry D. acquisition
    E. ordering

39. A master file of all registered borrowers in a library system is called the _____ file.
    A. personnel B. charging C. classification
    D. central registration E. circulation control

40. A person who charges out materials from a library is called the
    A. lender B. technician C. professional librarian D. clerk
    E. borrower

41. A catalog in which all entries are filed in alphabetical order is called a(n) _____ catalog.
    A. card B. Library of Congress C. alphabetical
    D. dictionary E. subject

42. The day material is to be returned to a library is usually referred to as the _____ day.
    A. library B. date-due C. return
    D. book E. library-due

43. The act of annulling the library's record of a loan is called
    A. discharging B. cancelling C. stamping D. recording
    E. unloaning

44. The penalty charge for material returned after the date   44. ___
    due is called a(n)
       A. charge   B. fine   C. tax   D. levy   E. arrangement

45. A set of materials containing rules designed to be played   45. ___
    in a competitive situation is called a
       A. rolodome   B. game   C. sketch   D. linedex
       E. materials-set

46. A catalog in more than one part is termed a _____ catalog.   46. ___
       A. divided   B. split   C. Library of Congress
       D. Dewey   E. Sears

47. A metal file containing a number of flat metal leaves that   47. ___
    hold single cardboard strips listing titles and holdings
    is called a
       A. linedesk   B. linetop   C. rolotop   D. rotofile
       E. linedex

48. A metal file containing a number of shallow drawers in   48. ___
    which serial check-in cards are kept is usually referred
    to as a
       A. linedesk   B. rotofile   B. box   D. kardex
       E. linetop

49. The strip of paper pasted in the book or on the book packet,   49. ___
    on which the date due is stamped, is called the
       A. date slip   B. date card   C. date strip
       D. call slip   E. card strip

50. Film on which materials have been photographed in greatly   50. ___
    reduced size is called
       A. minifilm   B. microfilm   C. photogram
       D. miniaturization   E. photoreduction

KEY (CORRECT ANSWERS)

1.	C	11.	A	21.	E	31.	E	41.	D
2.	D	12.	C	22.	A	32.	C	42.	B
3.	C	13.	C	23.	C	33.	E	43.	A
4.	A	14.	B	24.	B	34.	C	44.	B
5.	D	15.	A	25.	D	35.	B	45.	B
6.	B	16.	D	26.	B	36.	A	46.	A
7.	A	17.	D	27.	C	37.	B	47.	E
8.	E	18.	A	28.	C	38.	B	48.	D
9.	B	19.	C	29.	B	39.	D	49.	A
10.	A	20.	B	30.	B	40.	E	50.	B

EXAMINATION SECTION

TEST 1

DIRECTIONS: Each question or incomplete statement is followed by several suggested answers or completions. Select the one that BEST answers the question or completes the statement. *PRINT THE LETTER OF THE CORRECT ANSWER IN THE SPACE AT THE RIGHT.*

1. The items in a bibliography are arranged in
   A. alphabetical order according to the author's last name
   B. chronological order according to date of publication
   C. alphabetical order according to the first word in the title
   D. alphabetical order according to name of publisher

2. Which reference source would contain the MOST complete information on the British game of cricket?
   A. THE WORLD ALMANAC
   B. SKEAT'S ETYMOLOGICAL DICTIONARY
   C. READERS' GUIDE TO PERIODICAL LITERATURE
   D. ENCYCLOPEDIA BRITANNICA

3. How are novels arranged on a library shelf?
   A. Alphabetically by subject
   B. Alphabetically by author's last name
   C. Numerically by Dewey Decimal number
   D. Alphabetically by title

4. In the card catalog, cross reference cards are used PRIMARILY to
   A. locate a book on the shelves
   B. determine the author of a certain work
   C. locate additional information on a subject
   D. find other books by an author

5. Which would NOT be likely to appear on the editorial page of a newspaper?
   A. Readers' reactions   B. Masthead
   C. Syndicated columns   D. Classified ads

Questions 6-10.

DIRECTIONS: Questions 6 through 10 are based on the entry below from the READERS' GUIDE TO PERIODICAL LITERATURE. For each question, select the word or expression that BEST completes the statement or answers the question, and write its letter in the space at the right.

LITERARY prizes
  Added attraction; Seal Novel Awards for a first novel by a
    Canadian. P.S. Nathan. Pub W 216:26 D 3 '79
  Case of the two first novels: the Hemingway Award reexamined.
    S. Dong. Pub W 215:40+ Je 25 '79
  Consolation Prize; awarding of the Austrian State Prize for
    Literature to S. de Beauvoir. E. M. von Kuehnelt-Leddihn.
    Nat R 31:1040 Ag 17 '79
  Hasen wins Hemingway Award; figures suggest 1979 rise in
    published first novels. S. Dong. Pub W 215:17-18 Je 11 '79
  National Jewish Book Awards. Pub W 215:17 Je 11 '79
  1978: the year in review; literary prizes and awards.
    il Pub W 215:47-52 F 19 '79
  Tenth anniversary of the Freedley Memorial Award. D. B. Wilmeth.
    USA Today 108:66 Jl '79
  Three groups found awards for African heritage books.
    M. Reuter. Pub W 215:26+ Ap 2 '79
    See also
American Book Awards
Carey-Thomas Awards
National Book Awards
National Book Critics Circle Awards
Nobel prizes
Poetry - Awards
Pulitzer prizes
Scientific literature for children - Awards

6. In this entry on literary prizes, how are authors' names given?
   A. Last name only
   B. Last name and then first name
   C. First name and then last name
   D. Initials and then last name

7. According to this entry on literary prizes, which abbreviation does READERS' GUIDE use for *June*?
   A. J   B. Je   C. Jn   D. Ju

8. Under the heading *Literary prizes*, the entry *1978: the year in review* is listed
   A. chronologically   B. alphabetically
   C. by subject   D. by degree of importance

9. In the entry titled *Three groups found awards for African heritage books*, Ap 2 '79 refers to the date the
   A. magazine was published   B. award was given
   C. article was written   D. groups established the award

9.____

10. Which other article appears in the same issue of PUBLISHERS WEEKLY as *Hasen Wins Hemingway Award*?
    A. Added attraction
    B. Case of the two first novels
    C. National Jewish Book Awards
    D. 1978: the year in review

10.____

Questions 11-25.

DIRECTIONS: Listed below are some types of information you might want to locate together with several books in which you might look. For each write the letter of the BEST answer in the space at the right.

11. The officers and addresses of the regional and district officers of the Office of Price Administration may be found in
    A. CONGRESSIONAL DIRECTORY
    B. ENCYCLOPEDIA AMERICANA
    C. STATESMAN'S YEARBOOK
    D. GOVERNMENT MANUAL
    E. LARNED'S NEW HISTORY FOR READY REFERENCE

11.____

12. The current membership of the standing committees of the Senate may be found in
    A. ENCYCLOPEDIA AMERICANA
    B. CONGRESSIONAL DIRECTORY
    C. WORLD ALMANAC
    D. GOVERNMENTAL MANUAL
    E. STATESMAN'S YEARBOOK

12.____

13. The Washington addresses of the members of Congress may be found in
    A. WORLD ALMANAC   B. ENCYCLOPEDIA AMERICANA
    C. CONGRESSIONAL DIRECTORY   D. GOVERNMENT MANUAL
    E. STATESMAN'S YEARBOOK

13.____

14. To locate summaries of Franklin D. Roosevelt's speeches in 1942, one should consult
    A. WORLD ALMANAC   B. ENCYCLOPEDIA AMERICANA
    C. READERS' GUIDE   D. CURRENT BIOGRAPHY
    E. WHO'S WHO IN AMERICA

14.____

15. The definition of *Grossmann's law* may be found in Webster's NEW INTERNATIONAL DICTIONARY in
    A. new words section
    B. below the line in the main alphabet
    C. main alphabet
    D. Gazetteer
    E. biographical dictionary

15.____

16. The provisions and benefits of the New Zealand Social   16.___
    Security legislation of 1938 may be found in
        A. STATESMAN'S YEARBOOK
        B. LARNED'S NEW HISTORY FOR READY REFERENCE
        C. ENCYCLOPEDIA AMERICANA
        D. WORLD ALMANAC
        E. GOVERNMENT MANUAL

17. To find the location of the poem THE HIGHWAYMAN by   17.___
    Alfred Noyes, one would look in
        A. BARTLETT'S FAMILIAR QUOTATIONS
        B. COMPTON'S PICTURED ENCYCLOPEDIA
        C. ENCYCLOPEDIA AMERICANA
        D. THE WORLD BOOK
        E. GRANGER'S INDEX TO POETRY AND RECITATIONS

18. The biography of the Prime Minister of Great Britain may   18.___
    be found in
        A. WHO'S WHO IN AMERICA
        B. GRANGER'S INDEX TO POETRY AND RECITATIONS
        C. CURRENT BIOGRAPHY
        D. GROVE'S DICTIONARY OF MUSIC AND MUSICIANS

19. An account of Antarctic exploration featuring excerpts   19.___
    from scientific books and journals:
        A. LARNED'S NEW HISTORY FOR READY REFERENCE
        B. ENCYCLOPEDIA AMERICANA
        C. STATESMAN'S YEARBOOK
        D. GOVERNMENT MANUAL
        E. WORLD ALMANAC

20. The dates of Ash Wednesday and Easter Sunday from the   20.___
    year 1801 through 2000 may be found in
        A. COMPTON'S PICTURED ENCYCLOPEDIA
        B. LARNED'S NEW HISTORY FOR READY REFERENCE
        C. NEW INTERNATIONAL DICTIONARY
        D. WORLD ALMANAC
        E. STATESMAN'S YEARBOOK

21. The meaning of the letters D.A.G. may be found in the   21.___
    NEW STANDARD DICTIONARY in
        A. Key to abbreviations
        B. Statistics of population
        C. main alphabet
        D. Foreign words and phrases
        E. disputed pronunciations

22. To find the author of the poem beginning *"Thou are not   22.___
    lovelier than lilacs"*, look in
        A. GRANGER'S INDEX TO POETRY AND RECITATIONS
        B. COMPTON'S PICTURED ENCYCLOPEDIA
        C. BARTLETT'S FAMILIAR QUOTATIONS
        D. THE WORLD BOOK
        E. ENCYCLOPEDIA AMERICANA

23. The BOSTON MASSACRE may be found in WEBSTER'S NEW INTERNATIONAL DICTIONARY 2ND ED. in the
    A. main alphabet
    B. Gazetteer
    C. new words section
    D. main alphabet below the line
    E. biographical dictionary

24. A table showing the rank in population of the largest cities of the United States is the
    A. GOVERNMENT MANUAL
    B. CONGRESSIONAL DICTIONARY
    C. WORLD ALMANAC
    D. WEBSTER'S NEW INTERNATIONAL DICTIONARY

25. The definition of *coup d'etat* may be found in WEBSTER'S NEW INTERNATIONAL DICTIONARY in the
    A. Gazetteer
    B. new words
    C. pronouncing biographical dictionary
    D. WORLD ALMANAC
    E. main alphabet

KEY (CORRECT ANSWERS)

1. A
2. D
3. B
4. C
5. D

6. D
7. B
8. B
9. A
10. C

11. D
12. B
13. C
14. C
15. C

16. A
17. E
18. C
19. A
20. D

21. C
22. A
23. A
24. C
25. E

TEST 2

Questions 1-10.

DIRECTIONS: Listed below are some of the main headings of the Dewey decimal classification such as might appear on the library book shelves. Below the headings are ten topics on which you might want information. If you know under which heading each topic belongs, you could go *directly* to the shelf for the book you want. In the space at the right of each topic, write the number of the heading that BEST covers the topic. Use ONE number only for each topic and use *no* number more than once.

220	Bible	640	Home economics
290	Non-Christian religion	720	Architecture
320	Political science	730	Sculpture
330	Economics	750	Painting
350	Administration	760	Engraving
390	Customs and folklore	770	Photography
530	Physics	780	Music
540	Chemistry	800	Literature
550	Geology	910	Geography
580	Botany	913	Archaeology
590	Zoology	930	Ancient history
620	Engineering	942	English history
630	Agriculture	970	North American history

1. Hunting with a camera

2. Interior decoration

3. Excavations in the pyramids

4. A survey predicting the probability of oil

5. The poems of Robert Browning

6. The spread of representative government

7. A discussion of longitude and latitude

8. Classification of plants

9. A discussion of the technical points of bridge building

10. A copy of the picture, Mona Lisa, by Leonardo da Vinci

Questions 11-25.

DIRECTIONS: Each of the following statements lists a topic on which you might wish to find a book, together with the *possible* word under which to look for it in the card catalog. For each, write the letter of the BEST answer in the space at the right.

11. French revolution
    A. Napoleonic wars
    B. Reign of terror
    C. France - Revolution
    D. Revolution, French
    E. Terror, Reign of

    11._____

12. North American Indians
    A. Indians of North America
    B. Aborigines
    C. American aborigines
    D. American Indians
    E. Mounds and mound builders

    12._____

13. Democracy
    A. Democracy
    B. Free institutions
    C. Popular government
    D. Federal government
    E. Politics

    13._____

14. Soap carving
    A. Sculpture
    B. Soap sculpture
    C. Arts and crafts
    D. Fine Arts
    E. Handicrafts

    14._____

15. Business depressions
    A. Business cycles
    B. Economic cycles
    C. Stabilization in industry
    D. Economic conditions
    E. Depressions, Business

    15._____

16. Applied art
    A. Art industry and trade
    B. Decorative arts
    C. Industrial arts
    D. Arts and crafts movement
    E. Commercial art

    16._____

17. Prehistoric antiquities
    A. Antiquities
    B. Excavations
    C. Lake dwellers and lake dwellings
    D. Archaeology
    E. Ruins

    17._____

18. Conduits
    A. Aqueducts
    B. Water conduits
    C. Civil engineering
    D. Hydraulic engineering
    E. Water supply

    18._____

19. Actresses
    A. Actors and actresses
    B. Drama
    C. Theater
    D. Stage
    E. Acting

    19._____

20. Abolition of slavery
    A. American history
    B. Southern states
    C. Civil war
    D. Slavery
    E. Negroes

21. The 1984 platforms of both the Republican and Democratic political parties may be found in
    A. GOVERNMENT MANUAL
    B. CURRENT BIOGRAPHY
    C. ENCYCLOPEDIA AMERICANA
    D. LINCOLN LIBRARY
    E. WORLD ALMANAC

22. An authoritative bibliography for each country described is given in the
    A. WORLD ALMANAC
    B. GOVERNMENT MANUAL
    C. STATESMAN'S YEARBOOK
    D. CONGRESSIONAL DIRECTORY
    E. CURRENT BIOGRAPHY

23. To find the author and title of the poem beginning *"Dear charming, nymph, neglected and decried"*, look in
    A. COMPTON'S PICTURED ENCYCLOPEDIA
    B. BARTLETT'S FAMILIAR QUOTATIONS
    C. GRANGER'S INDEX TO POETRY AND RECITATION
    D. THE WORLD BOOK
    E. ENCYCLOPEDIA AMERICANA

24. A history of Alaska told by quotations (excerpts) from the writings of several historians may be found in
    A. STATESMAN'S YEARBOOK
    B. ENCYCLOPEDIA AMERICANA
    C. LARNED'S NEW HISTORY FOR READY REFERENCE
    D. WORLD ALMANAC
    E. CONGRESSIONAL DIRECTORY

25. A biographical note on Jane Addams may be found in the NEW STANDARD DICTIONARY in the
    A. main alphabet
    B. foreign words and phrases
    C. biographical section
    D. statistics of population
    E. rules for simplification of spelling

KEY (CORRECT ANSWERS)

1. 770	11. C
2. 640	12. A
3. 913	13. A
4. 550	14. B
5. 800	15. A
6. 320	16. A
7. 910	17. D
8. 580	18. A
9. 620	19. A
10. 750	20. D
21. E	
22. C	
23. C	
24. C	
25. A	

TEST 3

Questions 1-20.

DIRECTIONS: Each question consists of a statement. You are to indicate whether the statement is TRUE (T) or FALSE (F). *PRINT THE LETTER OF THE CORRECT ANSWER IN THE SPACE AT THE RIGHT.*

1. Biographies of poets may be found in GRANGER'S INDEX TO POETRY AND RECITATIONS. 1.____

2. To use THE LINCOLN LIBRARY OF ESSENTIAL INFORMATION, one should consult the index. 2.____

3. The words at the top of each page in the dictionary indicate the inclusive contents of the page. 3.____

4. THE STATESMAN'S YEARBOOK is published biennially. 4.____

5. The index is a valuable aid in the use of the ENCYCLOPAEDIA BRITANNICA. 5.____

6. The arrangement of BARTLETT'S FAMILIAR QUOTATIONS is chronological by author. 6.____

7. CURRENT BIOGRAPHY is arranged alphabetically. 7.____

8. The ENCYCLOPEDIA AMERICANA is arranged in large subject groups with an index. 8.____

9. WEBSTER'S NEW INTERNATIONAL DICTIONARY arranges all kinds of words in the English language in one alphabetical list. 9.____

10. Names of government officials may be found in the U.S. GOVERNMENT MANUAL. 10.____

11. WHO'S WHO IN AMERICA contains biographies of important people both living and dead. 11.____

12. COMPTON'S PICTURED ENCYCLOPEDIA is particularly good for children in the intermediate grades. 12.____

13. The articles in both the ENCYCLOPEDIA BRITANNICA and the ENCYCLOPEDIA AMERICANA are signed. 13.____

14. A feature of the NEW STANDARD DICTIONARY is the divided page by which obsolete words are given below the line. 14.____

15. The U.S. GOVERNMENT MANUAL contains biographies of government officials. 15.____

16. BARTLETT'S FAMILIAR QUOTATIONS contains complete poems. 16. ___

17. CURRENT BIOGRAPHY is published monthly and then cumulated. 17. ___

18. CURRENT BIOGRAPHY contains biographies of persons in the news. 18. ___

19. A description of the duties of the departments of the United States government will be found in the GOVERNMENT MANUAL. 19. ___

20. An encyclopedia should be consulted for the pronunciation of words. 20. ___

Questions 21-25.

DIRECTIONS: Listed below are some types of information you might want to locate, together with several books in which you might look. For each, write the letter of the BEST answer in the space at the right.

21. To find a list of magazine articles published in 1919 on the Versailles Treaty, you would consult 21. ___
    A. the ENCYCLOPAEDIA BRITANNICA
    B. THE READER'S GUIDE
    C. LARNED'S NEW HISTORY FOR READY REFERENCE
    D. the card catalog
    E. WEBSTER'S NEW INTERNATIONAL DICTIONARY

22. The purposes, powers, and personnel of the United States Government War Agencies of World War II may be found in the 22. ___
    A. CONGRESSIONAL DIRECTORY   B. GOVERNMENT MANUAL
    C. STATESMAN'S YEARBOOK   D. ENCYCLOPAEDIA BRITANNICA
    E. WORLD ALMANAC

23. A list of representative publications of departments and agencies of the federal government may be found in 23. ___
    A. LARNED'S NEW HISTORY FOR READY REFERENCE
    B. STATESMAN'S YEARBOOK
    C. GOVERNMENT MANUAL
    D. AMERICAN ENCYCLOPEDIA
    E. CONGRESSIONAL DIRECTORY

24. For a discussion of the life and works of Beethoven, one should consult 24. ___
    A. CURRENT BIOGRAPHY
    B. a daily newspaper
    C. GRANGER'S INDEX TO POETRY AND RECITATIONS
    D. GROVE'S DICTIONARY OF MUSIC AND MUSICIANS
    E. WHO'S WHO

25. The population of Topeka, Kansas, may be found in the NEW STANDARD DICTIONARY in the   25._____
    A. main alphabet
    B. foreign words and phrases
    C. disputed pronunciations
    D. key to abbreviations
    E. statistics of population

KEY (CORRECT ANSWERS)

1. F	11. F
2. T	12. T
3. T	13. T
4. F	14. F
5. T	15. F
6. T	16. F
7. T	17. T
8. F	18. T
9. F	19. T
10. T	20. F

21. B
22. B
23. C
24. D
25. E

EXAMINATION SECTION
TEST 1

DIRECTIONS: Each question or incomplete statement is followed by several suggested answers or completions. Select the one that BEST answers the question or completes the statement. *PRINT THE LETTER OF THE CORRECT ANSWER IN THE SPACE AT THE RIGHT.*

1. The BEST known encyclopedia in the Western world, first published in the 18th century, is

    A. WORLD BOOK ENCYCLOPEDIA
    B. COMPTON'S PICTURED ENCYCLOPEDIA
    C. ENCYCLOPEDIA BRITANNICA
    D. ENCYCLOPEDIA AMERICANA

    1.____

2. Authority-control records are important in an online catalog environment because they

    A. help prevent *blind* cross-references
    B. expand the capacity of the database
    C. keep the system from overloading
    D. provide access to fugitive materials

    2.____

3. The NEW ENCYCLOPEDIA BRITANNICA does NOT include the

    A. Micropaedia   B. Monopaedia
    C. Macropaedia   D. Propaedia

    3.____

4. Which of the following is NOT the name of an online catalog?

    A. Geobase   B. Dynix   C. Geac   D. OCLC

    4.____

5. Nom de plume is synonymous with

    A. pseudonym   B. nickname
    C. given name   D. telonism

    5.____

6. Component-word searching is another way of saying _____ searching.

    A. key-word   B. permuterm
    C. subject   D. author/title

    6.____

7. The ENCYCLOPEDIA AMERICANA is ESPECIALLY useful for

    A. finding information about movie stars
    B. finding little-known material about the United States
    C. finding tide charts
    D. doing comprehensive world research

    7.____

8. The citation indexes (SCIENCE CITATION INDEX, etc.) are unique in that they

    A. allow searching by the name of an institution
    B. provide access to foreign language journals
    C. allow searching of an author's references
    D. contain millions of unique records

    8.____

9. The following are all children's and young adults' encyclopedias EXCEPT

    A. MERIT STUDENTS ENCYCLOPEDIA
    B. WORLD BOOK ENCYCLOPEDIA
    C. COMPTON'S ENCYCLOPEDIA AND FACT BOOK
    D. COLLIER'S ENCYCLOPEDIA

10. A good online public access catalog (OPAC) can be expected to provide all of the following EXCEPT

    A. author and title access to books and audio-visual materials
    B. the loan status of materials that circulate
    C. information regarding who a book has been loaned to
    D. the place and publisher of each book in the catalog

11. Of the points to consider in a systematic evaluation of an encyclopedia, the LEAST important one is

    A. cost
    B. viewpoint and objectivity
    C. subject coverage
    D. number of pages

12. Widespread searching of bibliographic databases dates back to

    A. the 1950's
    B. 1960
    C. the mid-1980's
    D. the early 1970's

13. The format of a reference set means the

    A. writing style
    B. binding and size
    C. authority of contributors
    D. viewpoint and objectivity

14. The FIRST bibliographic databases were by-products of

    A. progress in NASA technology
    B. online card catalogs such as OCLC
    C. information dissemination centers
    D. the computerized typesetting operation

15. A patron asks your advice as a librarian on a set of encyclopedias he is considering for his family.
    The MOST helpful response for you is to

    A. give limited advice and provide the patron with professional reviews of the set under question
    B. give no advice for fear of repercussions from sales-persons and publishers
    C. endorse or condemn the set whole-heartedly, depending on your own opinion
    D. refer the patron to the director of the library

16. The four basic components of the online industry include all of the following EXCEPT

    A. libraries and information centers
    B. library school administrators
    C. end-users who request information
    D. database producers

17. McGraw-Hill's ENCYCLOPEDIA OF WORLD ART is an example of a _____ encyclopedia.

    A. children's
    B. subject
    C. supermarket
    D. foreign

18. Which of the following bibliographic databases is NOT produced by a federal government agency or federally-supported institution?

    A. ERIC   B. COMPENDEX   C. AGRICOLA   D. MEDLINE

19. A ready-reference work is one which

    A. is allowed to circulate outside of the library
    B. is especially difficult to use
    C. arrives on a monthly basis
    D. is useful for *quick* questions of a factual nature

20. All of the following are examples of source documents EXCEPT

    A. patents
    B. conference papers
    C. indexes
    D. newspapers

21. The STATISTICAL ABSTRACT OF THE UNITED STATES is a compendium in the sense that it

    A. contains statistics on a wide range of subjects
    B. is published on an annual basis
    C. is a summary of U.S. Census data
    D. can be used for research in education

22. The number EJ121478, as part of an ERIC record, would indicate that the material referenced

    A. is a journal article
    B. is a book
    C. is an ERIC document on microfiche
    D. was entered in the database in 1978

23. Which of the following almanacs is published in London, England?

    A. WHITAKER'S ALMANAC
    B. INFORMATION PLEASE ALMANAC
    C. WORLD ALMANAC AND BOOK OF FACTS
    D. THE PEOPLE'S ALMANAC

24. A thesaurus which accompanies an index such as ERIC is a list of

    A. corporate authors
    B. journals indexed
    C. stop words
    D. assigned descriptors

25. Ready-reference materials include all of the following EXCEPT

    A. STATISTICAL ABSTRACT OF THE UNITED STATES
    B. INFORMATION PLEASE ALMANAC
    C. BIOLOGICAL ABSTRACTS
    D. THE NEW YORK RED BOOK

KEY (CORRECT ANSWERS)

1. C
2. A
3. B
4. A
5. A

6. A
7. B
8. C
9. D
10. C

11. D
12. D
13. B
14. D
15. A

16. B
17. B
18. B
19. D
20. C

21. C
22. A
23. A
24. D
25. C

———

TEST 2

DIRECTIONS: Each question or incomplete statement is followed by several suggested answers or completions. Select the one that BEST answers the question or completes the statement. *PRINT THE LETTER OF THE CORRECT ANSWER IN THE SPACE AT THE RIGHT.*

1. The U.S. National Library of Medicine produces all of the following databases EXCEPT

    A. EMBASE   B. AIDSLINE   C. CANCERLIT   D. MEDLINE

2. H.W. Wilson's CURRENT BIOGRAPHY provides

    A. essay-length biographical information
    B. reference to information in BIOGRAPHY INDEX
    C. no more information on an individual than is provided by WHO'S WHO
    D. reviews of best-selling biographies

3. The database which provides access to fugitive materials in education is

    A. Academic Index
    B. Education Index
    C. ERIC
    D. Mental Measurements Yearbook

4. All of the following are covered in CONTEMPORARY AUTHORS EXCEPT

    A. screenwriters   B. poets
    C. dramatists   D. technical writers

5. Boolean logic utilizes all of the following logical operators EXCEPT

    A. if   B. or   C. not   D. and

6. A prescriptive dictionary is one which

    A. discusses in great detail the origin of a word
    B. adheres to tradition and historical authority for word definitions and approved usage
    C. attempts to relate every possible definition and usage of a word
    D. is published only in the United States

7. Free-text searching in a bibliographic database means

    A. searching several descriptors at one time
    B. using Boolean logic in your search
    C. searching without the use of controlled vocabulary
    D. searching only titles and abstracts

8. ABRIDGED INDEX MEDICUS differs from INDEX MEDICUS in that it

    A. contains citations to English-language journals only
    B. contains only information from the last twelve months
    C. contains citations to foreign-language journals only
    D. is not published by the National Library of Medicine

1. ____
2. ____
3. ____
4. ____
5. ____
6. ____
7. ____
8. ____

9. The two PRINCIPAL operations of public services are

   A. circulation and reference
   B. reference and serials management
   C. circulation and collection development
   D. reference and classification

10. Of the following reasons for an academic library to acquire the DICTIONARY OF AMERICAN SLANG, which is the LEAST valid?

   A. Most regular dictionaries do not indicate the variations of meaning of given slang terms or words.
   B. Students often come across expressions which are not defined well in ordinary dictionaries.
   C. It is a good source to check on the language used by an author to convey a character's background or social class.
   D. Students and librarians alike enjoy reading through it during their leisure time.

11. Collection maintenance includes all of the following EXCEPT

   A. taking inventory
   B. reshelving books
   C. identifying overdues
   D. shelf-reading

12. A gazetteer is a

   A. biographical dictionary
   B. good source for looking up phases of the moon
   C. geographical dictionary
   D. guide to motels throughout the United States

13. A Dewey Decimal Classification number never has MORE than how many digits to the LEFT of the decimal?

   A. Four   B. Five   C. Three   D. Two

14. In MOST government depository libraries, the government documents are arranged on the shelves

   A. by Superintendent of Documents numbers
   B. by Library of Congress call numbers
   C. by Dewey Decimal numbers
   D. alphabetically by title

15. The Library of Congress Classification System is different from the Dewey Decimal Classification System in that it

   A. arranges books on the shelf by subject
   B. does not include author numbers
   C. is not frequently used by libraries in the United States
   D. was developed to meet the needs of a specific library's collection

16. The BEST reference source for finding, in detail, the organization and activities of all U.S. government agencies is

    A. POLITICS IN AMERICA
    B. THE STATESMAN'S YEARBOOK
    C. UNITED STATES GOVERNMENT MANUAL
    D. MOODY'S MUNICIPAL AND GOVERNMENT MANUAL

17. The added entries in a catalog record could be for

    A. joint authors, titles, or series
    B. joint authors, series, or subjects
    C. joint authors, titles, or subjects
    D. titles, publishers, or series

18. Which of the following illustrates a directional question?

    A. How far is Syracuse from Lake Ontario?
    B. Where is the public telephone?
    C. Where can I find a biographical dictionary of presidents?
    D. Is Italy to the east of Spain?

19. You are performing an online bibliographic search for a patron and have brought up a set consisting of 300 records.
    Of the following, which is the LEAST valid way of limiting the search in order to avoid printing such a large set?

    A. Limit the search to a certain range of years
    B. Redefine the search using more specific descriptors
    C. Print only the first 40 records of the set
    D. Cut out references to articles in languages the patron cannot read

20. All of the following are examples of primary sources EXCEPT

    A. diaries
    B. biographies
    C. letters
    D. memoirs

21. *What is the population of Mexico City?* would MOST likely be classified as what type of reference question?

    A. Ready reference
    B. Directional
    C. Research on a topic
    D. Instructional

22. Something you would NOT expect to find in a vertical file is

    A. a monograph
    B. a pamphlet
    C. a folded map
    D. newspaper clippings

23. Logical product, logical sum, and logical difference are all part of what type of searching?

    A. Permuterm logic
    B. Keyword-in-context (KWIC)
    C. Statistical logic
    D. Boolean logic

24. Keyword-in-context (KWIC) indexing is also called _____ indexing.

    A. title
    B. comprehensive
    C. subject
    D. permutation

25. The MARC format was developed at the
   A. National Library of Medicine
   B. British Library
   C. Library of Congress
   D. Smithsonian Institute

26. Patrons of a general library are usually MOST aware of which of the following library activities?
   A. Circulation
   B. Accession
   C. Cataloging
   D. Reference

27. Three of the following four are consequences of the copy-righting of books by the U.S. government.
   Which is NOT such a consequence?
   A. Protecting author's rights
   B. Encouraging writing
   C. Securing deposit material for the government
   D. Government endorsement of the copyrighted texts

28. The term *cataloging in publication* refers to a cataloging program under which cataloging information
   A. appears in the PUBLISHERS' WEEKLY
   B. appears in the National Union Catalog
   C. appears in the publication itself
   D. is prepared by the publisher

29. The MAJOR use of a formal statement of a library's objective is
   A. serving as a guideline for program development and services
   B. justifying library staffing to the board and public
   C. convincing the governing body of the need for financial support
   D. training library staff in improved methods and practices

30. Circulation statistics should be gathered PRIMARILY for the purpose of
   A. justifying the library budget
   B. improving library service
   C. cutting library costs
   D. analyzing personnel performance

KEY (CORRECT ANSWERS)

1. A
2. A
3. C
4. D
5. A

6. B
7. C
8. A
9. A
10. D

11. C
12. C
13. C
14. A
15. D

16. C
17. A
18. B
19. C
20. B

21. A
22. A
23. D
24. D
25. C

26. A
27. D
28. C
29. A
30. B

TEST 3

DIRECTIONS: Each question or incomplete statement is followed by several suggested answers or completions. Select the one that BEST answers the question or completes the statement. *PRINT THE LETTER OF THE CORRECT ANSWER IN THE SPACE AT THE RIGHT.*

1. A typical reference in the READER'S GUIDE TO PERIODICAL LITERATURE would include all of the following EXCEPT

   A. author
   B. title of the article
   C. journal name
   D. journal abstract

   1.___

2. An example of a subject authority list used in cataloging is the

   A. THESAURUS OF ERIC DESCRIPTORS
   B. LIBRARY OF CONGRESS SUBJECT HEADINGS
   C. NEW YORK TIMES INDEX
   D. CINAHL SUBJECT HEADING LIST

   2.___

3. An example of a nonperiodical serial is

   A. EUROPA YEARBOOK
   B. AQUACULTURE MAGAZINE
   C. THE WASHINGTON POST
   D. JOURNAL OF THE AMERICAN MEDICAL ASSOCIATION

   3.___

4. The Superintendent of Documents classification system arranges government documents on the shelves

   A. alphabetically by title
   B. by government agency
   C. alphabetically by author
   D. according to date of printing

   4.___

5. Which of the following is an example of an open-ended question?

   A. Would you like books or magazine articles?
   B. You say you need to know the elevation of Denver?
   C. What kind of information about sharks are you looking for?
   D. Have you ever used our online catalog?

   5.___

6. Scientific Information's weekly CURRENT CONTENTS consists of

   A. reproductions of journal contents pages
   B. a subject index for scientific journals
   C. author and title indexes for current periodicals
   D. scientific journal abstracts

   6.___

7. All of the following are bibliographic utilities involved in resource sharing EXCEPT

   A. OCLC   B. RLIN   C. DYNIX   D. UTLAS

   7.___

8. The MAIN objective of reference negotiation is to

   A. save the librarian's time
   B. steer patrons away from heavily used sources
   C. find out what the patron specifically needs
   D. instruct patrons in the proper use of reference materials

9. Which of the following PROPERLY demonstrates a logical product and logical difference search statement?

   A. Dogs and cats, not birds
   B. (Dogs or cats) and not birds
   C. Dogs and not birds or cats
   D. Dogs and (cats or birds)

10. The generally accepted definition of a serial includes all of the following EXCEPT

    A. yearbooks
    B. newspapers
    C. theses
    D. journals

11. ESSAY AND GENERAL LITERATURE INDEX is MOST useful for locating

    A. a specific chapter of a book
    B. magazine and journal articles
    C. biographical essays
    D. a pamphlet or newsletter

12. What do LIBRARY JOURNAL, SHEEHY'S GUIDE TO REFERENCE BOOKS, and ARBA have in common?
    They

    A. are all periodicals
    B. discuss management of online catalogs
    C. provide critical evaluation of reference materials
    D. discuss only highly recommended reference sources

13. SHORT STORY INDEX covers stories published

    A. on all subjects except science fiction
    B. in collections and the NEW YORK TIMES
    C. in collections and periodicals
    D. by American authors only

14. One way in which nonperiodical serials (such as yearbooks) are different from periodical serials (such as journals) is that nonperiodicals are

    A. published several times a year
    B. usually a collection of articles
    C. usually ordered by subscription
    D. usually acquired through a standing order

15. Of the general serial sources listed below, which is the only one that includes newspapers?

    A. STANDARD PERIODICAL DIRECTORY
    B. GALE DIRECTORY OF PUBLICATIONS
    C. ULRICH'S INTERNATIONAL PERIODICALS DIRECTORY
    D. IRREGULAR SERIALS AND ANNUALS

16. The READER'S GUIDE TO PERIODICAL LITERATURE indexes

    A. magazines and newspapers
    B. popular magazines
    C. scholarly journals
    D. short story anthologies

17. Ethnic numbers are added to classification symbols so as to arrange books by

    A. subject   B. place of printing
    C. author   D. language

18. End-matter items could include all of the following EXCEPT

    A. appendices   B. bibliographies
    C. tables of contents   D. indexes

19. Which of the following BEST describes a jobber?
    A

    A. company which produces databases
    B. corporate body responsible for placing a book on the market
    C. wholesale bookseller who stocks books and supplies them to libraries
    D. person skilled in writing computer programs

20. The word *an* is a stopword on the Medline database.
    This means that

    A. it cannot be used as a search term in the database
    B. Medline includes articles such as *an* and *the* when alphabetizing by title
    C. if you type in that word, you will exit the database
    D. you cannot use Medline when searching for a title that begins with *an*

21. Of the following queries, which could NOT be answered by consulting a regular dictionary?

    A. What is the Golden Rule?
    B. How deep is a fathom?
    C. Does "humble" come from the same root as "human"?
    D. What are the rules for writing a sonnet?

22. An accurate definition of annals would be a(n)

    A. serial publication issued once a year
    B. anonymous publication
    C. record of events arranged in chronological order
    D. bibliography of an author's writings arranged by date of publication

23. West's FEDERAL PRACTICE DIGEST is an index to

    A. United States Supreme Court cases
    B. United States statutes
    C. New York State statutes
    D. The Code of Federal Regulations

24. MOST federal government documents are printed by

    A. the Government Printing Office
    B. the Library of Congress
    C. the United States Printing Office
    D. Congress

25. Setting aside a separate section for oversized books is an example of

    A. subject cataloging
    B. parallel arrangement
    C. a special materials collection
    D. Dewey Decimal Classification

KEY (CORRECT ANSWERS)

1.	D	11.	A
2.	B	12.	C
3.	A	13.	C
4.	B	14.	D
5.	C	15.	B
6.	A	16.	B
7.	C	17.	D
8.	C	18.	C
9.	A	19.	C
10.	C	20.	A

21.	D
22.	C
23.	A
24.	A
25.	B

EXAMINATION SECTION
TEST 1

DIRECTIONS: Each question or incomplete statement is followed by several suggested answers or completions. Select the one that BEST answers the question or completes the statement. *PRINT THE LETTER OF THE CORRECT ANSWER IN THE SPACE AT THE RIGHT.*

1. The MOST fundamental obligation of any museum is
    A. publicity
    B. raising funds
    C. collecting
    D. preparing exhibits

2. Which of the following design elements is MOST characteristic of an art/archaeology museum?
    A. Large, cumbersome showcases
    B. Long, narrow viewing rooms
    C. Large, numerous storerooms
    D. Strong artificial lighting

3. It is generally thought that a room in a museum intended for temporary exhibits and lectures should NOT be
    A. included in the itinerary normally followed by visitors
    B. close to or leading directly off of the entrance hall
    C. fully equipped with safety devices
    D. as large as possible

4. Of the following, a(n) _____ would MOST likely be classified as a superorganic museum object.
    A. bower-bird nest
    B. Aztec figurine
    C. bonzai tree
    D. coal deposit sample

5. The relative humidity which is considered to be the upper limit for the safety of organic material in a museum is _____%.
    A. 20
    B. 35
    C. 50
    D. 70

6. The museum administrator who takes charge of specific collections is the
    A. director
    B. clerk
    C. curator
    D. trustee

7. The _____ approach to the development of museum exhibits is generally acknowledged to be the MOST effective.
    A. open storage
    B. combined
    C. idea
    D. object

8. The architecture of a museum has, as its FIRST obligation, the accommodation of the needs of its
    A. exhibits
    B. visitors
    C. objects
    D. donors

9. Which of the following is NOT included among the principles of historic preservation?
   A. Planning by interpreters in conjunction with directors
   B. Clarity of purpose, possibilities, and limitations
   C. Strong emphasis on research
   D. Preservation of as many buildings and objects as possible from the past

10. Which of the following types of objects is MOST likely to be useful to a history museum?
    A. Relics
    B. Unique, one-of-a-kind objects
    C. Personal memorabilia
    D. Common, everyday artifacts

11. The source of museum income that is LEAST likely to be among the most productive is
    A. admission fees
    B. endowment funds
    C. graduated membership fees
    D. privately offered grants

12. The MAIN difference between the practices of inventory and cataloguing objects in a museum is that inventory is
    A. more subject to variation
    B. primarily administrative
    C. not comprehensive
    D. usually scientific

13. A DISADVANTAGE associated with the use of overhead lighting in museums is
    A. increased architectural and technical problems
    B. decreased effectiveness of security measures
    C. limited light supply
    D. difficulty in regulating light intensity

14. Costs of security measures for museum collections should be weighed against each of the following EXCEPT the _____ the objects.
    A. possibility of replacing
    B. public esteem of
    C. monetary value of
    D. scientific, historical, or interpretive importance of

15. What is generally considered by museologists to be the MOST important consideration in the administration of a museum?
    A. Cleanliness   B. Security
    C. Publicity   D. Accessibility

16. Which of the following security devices for use within the museum building is usually the LEAST expensive to operate and maintain?
    A. Sound detector   B. Pressure switch pad
    C. Photoelectric cells D. Ultrasonic detector

17. The SAFEST way to store framed pictures in an art museum is to
    A. lay them flat in closed specimen cabinets
    B. hang them on metal mesh panels
    C. stack them with intermittent layers of acid-free paper
    D. lay them flat on open shelved panels

18. The keeping of something that exists and safeguarding it from further change is the practice of
    A. refurbishment   B. restoration
    C. reconstruction   D. preservation

19. The classification of each museum object according to its subject is known as
    A. cataloguing   B. registration
    C. listing   D. accession

20. The general rule among MOST museums is to direct _____ of the annual operating budget to staff salaries.
    A. 1/6   B. 1/4   C. 1/2   D. 2/3

21. According to the generally accepted staffing patterns of a large city's municipal art and history museum, a maintenance person would operate under the direct leadership of the
    A. curator of collections   B. director
    C. curator of exhibits   D. assistant director

22. Which of the following would NOT be classified as a biological museum object?
    A(n)
    A. ant colony   B. insectivorous plant
    C. wave exhibit   D. trilobite fossil

23. _____ is NOT considered to be one of the MAIN limiting factors in deciding the selection of objects for use and display in a museum.
    A. Geography   B. Cost
    C. Time   D. Use

24. The ULTIMATE purpose of any museum is
    A. education   B. research
    C. collection   D. reference

25. The chief administrative officer of a museum, who is responsible for conducting all museum operations, including personnel, is the
    A. director   B. curator   C. trustee   D. docent

KEY (CORRECT ANSWERS)

1. C
2. B
3. A
4. B
5. D

6. C
7. B
8. C
9. D
10. D

11. C
12. B
13. A
14. B
15. B

16. B
17. B
18. D
19. A
20. D

21. D
22. C
23. B
24. A
25. A

TEST 2

DIRECTIONS: Each question or incomplete statement is followed by several suggested answers or completions. Select the one that BEST answers the question or completes the statement. *PRINT THE LETTER OF THE CORRECT ANSWER IN THE SPACE AT THE RIGHT.*

1. What is considered by museologists to be the starting point for making decisions concerning any museum activity?
    A. Purpose
    B. Collections
    C. Objects
    D. Staff capacity

    1.___

2. Which of the following items of information is NOT usually included in a museum's catalogue file?
    A. Number of objects received from each donor source
    B. Photographs of each object
    C. Object's museum location
    D. Value of each object

    2.___

3. In the _____ approach to the development of museum exhibits, display items are chosen BEFORE any other decisions are made.
    A. idea
    B. open storage
    C. combined
    D. object

    3.___

4. The design characteristic MOST likely to be included in the construction of a museum devoted to science and technology is
    A. inset showcases
    B. strong artificial lighting
    C. wide variety in room size
    D. large, centralized storage space

    4.___

5. As a general rule, museum objects that are stored and preserved in liquid should be inspected
    A. weekly
    B. monthly
    C. every six months
    D. annually

    5.___

6. Of the following, a _____ would be classified as an inorganic museum object.
    A. marble sculpture
    B. crystal geode
    C. caged animal
    D. mounted butterfly

    6.___

7. Which of the following is NOT one of the methods generally practiced for eliminating an object from a museum's collection?
    A. Return to donor
    B. Destruction
    C. Return to field site
    D. Sale

    7.___

8. The method for guiding visitors through museums which is MOST likely to create traffic problems among viewers is
   A. labels
   B. leaflets
   C. personal guides
   D. audio-visual equipment

9. The MOST frequently advocated alternative to refurnishing historical structures is
   A. stage setting
   B. sound and light effects
   C. symbolism
   D. adaptive occupancy

10. In a small museum, the _____ is generally hired in the third stage of hiring.
    A. secretary   B. curator   C. director   D. guard

11. Which of the following methods for building a museum collection is MOST likely to be part of a passive collecting program?
    A. Expedition/field collecting
    B. Transfer
    C. Donation
    D. Purchase

12. The person responsible for developing an educational exhibit should first concern him/herself primarily with each of the following EXCEPT
    A. abstracting
    B. selecting objects
    C. simplifying
    D. insuring interest

13. During the development of a furnished historic structure, which of the following stages would occur FIRST?
    A. Listing classified structures
    B. Master plan
    C. Planning directive
    D. Construction drawings

14. The term for any object that is shaped, produced, or selected for use by human workmanship is
    A. specimen   B. artifact   C. antique   D. heirloom

15. The MOST important factor in deciding what to keep or reject in the collection of a history museum is
    A. available funds
    B. museum size
    C. historical facts of the region
    D. popular culture

16. According to the generally accepted staffing patterns of a large city's municipal art and history museum, a draftsman/artist would operate under the direct leadership of the
    A. curator of collections
    B. director
    C. curator of exhibits
    D. assistant director

17. In terms of historic preservation, the practice of _____ takes on the specific responsibility of returning an existing building to its original appearance and condition.
    A. restoration
    B. refurbishment
    C. reconstruction
    D. refurnishment

18. In caring for an historic structure that is being used as an exhibit, which of the following is generally considered to be a monthly task?
    A. Dusting exhibit room furnishings
    B. Cleaning walls of exhibit rooms
    C. Stripping and waxing exhibit room wood floors
    D. Cleaning rugs of exhibit rooms

19. The PRIMARY purpose for a public museum's collections is
    A. visual aids in public lectures
    B. reference
    C. research
    D. exhibits

20. The security measures of a museum should be directed PRIMARILY toward
    A. acquiring trained and knowledgeable guard personnel
    B. controlling climatic conditions within the museum facility
    C. providing adequate insurance against loss
    D. preventing loss of any kind from any source

21. Of all the means of interpretation that operate during a visit to an historical museum, the MOST important is the
    A. accompanying literature or leaflet
    B. verbal narration of a personal guide
    C. placement and wording of labels
    D. furnished structure exhibit

22. Museums whose collections embrace a large number of fields are described as
    A. cross-referenced
    B. omnologous
    C. heterogeneous
    D. encyclopedic

23. Each of the following is a purpose of museum inventory EXCEPT
    A. facilitating scientific interpretation of uncatalogued objects
    B. providing background data for the catalogue
    C. providing a detailed description of each object for the catalogue
    D. ensuring consistent identification numbers for all succeeding catalogues

24. Large showcases are MOST likely to predominate the design of a(n) _____ museum.
    A. art/archaeology
    B. ethnographic/folk
    C. historical/archival
    D. science/technology

25. The museum administrator who is responsible for financing the museum and drafting broad policy is the
   A. director   B. registrar   C. trustee   D. curator

KEY (CORRECT ANSWERS)

1. C
2. A
3. D
4. C
5. C

6. B
7. C
8. A
9. D
10. D

11. C
12. B
13. A
14. B
15. C

16. C
17. A
18. B
19. C
20. D

21. D
22. D
23. C
24. B
25. C

EXAMINATION SECTION
TEST 1

Directions: Each question or incomplete statement is followed by several suggested answers or completions. Select the one that BEST answers the question or completes the statement. *PRINT THE LETTER OF THE CORRECT ANSWER IN THE SPACE AT THE RIGHT.*

1) A specialist is meeting with a panel of local community leaders to determine their perceptions about the effectiveness of a recent outreach program. The leaders seem unresponsive to the specialist's questions, looking at the floor or each other without directly answering the specialist's questions. One strategy that might work to elicit the desired information would be to

A. try to discern the hidden meaning of their silence
B. adopt a mildly confrontational tone and remind them of what's at stake in the community
C. keep asking open-ended questions and wait patiently for responses
D. tell them to come back when they're ready to tell you their opinions

1. _____

2) Each of the following statements about maintaining a community's attention is true, EXCEPT

A. The more challenging it is to pay attention to a message, the more likely it is that it will be attended to.
B. Listeners will be more motivated to pay attention if a speech is personally meaningful.
C. People will be more likely to attend if a speaker pauses to suggest natural transitions in a speech.
D. Listeners will attend to messages that stand out.

2. _____

3) Each of the following is a key strategy to integrative bargaining among community members in conflict, EXCEPT

A. focusing on positions, rather than interests
B. separating the people from the problem
C. aiming for an outcome based on an objectively identified standard
D. using active listening skills, such as rephrasing and questioning

3. _____

4) Which of the following is NOT one of the major variables to take into account when considering a community needs assessment?

A. State of program development
B. Resources available
C. Demographics
D. Community attitudes

4. _____

5) Which of the following groups would probably be formed specifically for, or be involved in, the purpose of addressing a specific unmet community need?

5. _____

A. An existing consumer group
B. A council of community representatives
C. A committee
D. An existing community organization

6) If a public outreach campaign designed to mobilize a community fails, the most likely reason for this failure is that the campaign

6. _____

A. was not specific about what they want people to do
B. are overly serious and do not appeal to people's sense of humor
C. offered no incentive for the audience to make a change
D. did not use language that appealed to the audience's emotions

7) Nationwide, the rate of involvement of elderly people in community-based programs demonstrates that they are

7. _____

A. underserved when compared to other age groups
B. served at about the same rate as other age groups
C. over-served when compared to other age groups
D. hardly served at all

8) In projecting the likelihood of an education program's success, a domestic violence specialist identifies every single event that must occur to complete the project. The specialist then arranges these events in sequential order and allocates time requirements for each. Finally, the total time is calculated and a model showing all their events and timelines is charted. The specialist has used

8. _____

A. a PERT chart
B. a simulation
C. a Markov model
D. the critical path method

9) When working with members of a predominantly African-American community, specialists from other cultural backgrounds should be aware that African Americans tend to express thoughts and feelings through descriptions of

9. _____

A. physically tangible sensations
B. problems to be analyzed
C. corresponding analogies
D. spiritual issues

10) Local nonprofessionals should be considered useful to a specialist who is looking to undertake a community outreach or educational initiative. Which of the following is LEAST likely to be a characteristic or role demonstrated by these community members?

10. _____

A. Undertaking support functions at the agency
B. Serving as a communication channel between the agency and clients
C. Encouraging greater agency acceptance and credibility within the community
D. Helping the agency to accomplish meaningful change

11) In working with Native American groups or clients, it is important to recognize that the greatest health problem facing their communities today is

11. _____

A. domestic violence
B. depression and suicide
C. alcoholism
D. tuberculosis

12) A specialist is facilitating a cooperative conflict resolution session between community members who have different opinions about what kinds of intervention services should be offered by the local adult protective services agency. Which of the following is NOT a guideline that should be followed in this process?

12. _____

A. Early in the negotiations, ask each party to name the issues on which they will positively not yield.
B. Try to get the parties to view the issue from other points of view, beside the two or three conflicting ones.
C. Have each side volunteer what it would be willing to do to resolve the conflict.
D. At the end of the session, draw up a formal agreement with agreed-upon actions for both parties.

13) A specialist wants to evaluate the effectiveness of a local women's shelter. The shelter has suffered from lax participation, given the number of women who have been abused in the surrounding area. The specialist wants to speak with the women in the community who did not follow up on referrals to the shelter, and begins by visiting some of these women. After gaining the trust of these women, the specialist asks for the names of women they know who might be in need of help with a domestic violence situation. The specialist's approach in this case is _____ sampling.

13. _____

A. maximum variation
B. snowball
C. convenience
D. typical case

14) When it comes to perceiving messages, people typically DON'T

A. tend to simplify causal connections and sometimes even seek a single cause to explain what may be a highly complex effect
B. tend to perceive messages independently of a categorical framework, especially if the message may be distorted by such an interpretation
C. have a predisposition toward accepting any pattern that a speaker offers to explain seemingly unconnected facts
D. tend to interpret things in the way they are viewed by their reference group

15) The elder members of Native American communities, regardless of kinship, are most commonly referred to as

A. the ancients
B. father or mother
C. grandfather or grandmother
D. chiefs

16) Each of the following is typically an objective of community mobilization, EXCEPT

A. To convince existing community resources to alter their services or work together to address an unmet need
B. To gather and distribute information to consumers and agencies about unmet needs
C. To publicize existing community resources and make them more accessible
D. To bring an unmet community need to public attention in order to achieve acceptance of and support for fulfilling the need

17) Research in community outreach shows that women often build friendships through shared positive feelings, whereas men often build friendships through

A. metacommunication
B. catharsis
C. impression management
D. shared activities

18) Typically, the FIRST step in a community needs assessment is to

A. identify community's strengths
B. explore the nature of the neighborhood
C. get to know the area and its residents
D. talk to people in the community

19) Most public relations experts agree that _____ exposure(s) to a message is the minimum just to get the message noticed. If the aim of a public outreach campaign is action or a change in behavior, the agency budget must plan for more exposures.

19. _____

A. one
B. two
C. three
D. four

20) In the program development/community liaison model of community work and public outreach, the primary constituency is considered to be

20. _____

A. community representatives and the service agency board or administrators
B. elected officials, social agencies, and interagency organizations
C. marginalized or oppressed population groups in a city or region
D. residents of a neighborhood, parish or rural county

21) Social or interpersonal problems in many African American communities have their roots in

21. _____

A. personality deficits
B. unresolved family conflicts
C. poor communication
D. external stressors

22) A public outreach campaign should

22. _____

  I. focus on short-term, measurable goals, rather than ultimate outcomes
  II. try to alter entrenched attitudes within a short time, with powerfully worded messages
  III. proceed in steps or phases, each of which lays out a mechanism that leads to the desired effect
  IV. ignore causes that led to a problem, and instead focus on solutions

A. I and II
B. II and III
C. III only
D. I, II, III and IV

23) Research findings indicate that in listing preferences for helping professional attributes, individuals from culturally diverse groups are MOST likely to _____ as more important than _____.

A. personality similarity; either race/ethnic similarity or attitude similarity
B. therapist experience; any kind of similarity
C. race/ethnic similarity; attitude similarity
D. attitude similarity; race/ethnic similarity

23. _____

24) Each of the following is considered to be an objective of community organization, EXCEPT

A. effecting changes in the distribution of decision-making power
B. helping people develop and strengthen the traits of self-direction and cooperation
C. effecting and maintaining the balance between needs and resources in a community
D. helping people deal with their problems by developing alternative behaviors

24. _____

25) A specialist is helping the adult protective services agency to design a public outreach campaign. The topic to be addressed is complex, public understanding is low, and most professionals at the agency feel that having more complete information might change the opinions of community members. Which method of pre-campaign research is probably most appropriate?

A. Deliberative polling
B. Attitude scales
C. Surveys or questionnaires
D. Focus groups

25. _____

KEY (CORRECT ANSWERS)

1. C
2. A
3. A
4. C
5. C

6. A
7. A
8. D
9. C
10. A

11. C
12. A
13. B
14. B
15. C

16. B
17. D
18. B
19. C
20. A

21. D
22. C
23. D
24. D
25. A

TEST 2

Directions: Each question or incomplete statement is followed by several suggested answers or completions. Select the one the BEST answers the question or completes the statement. *PRINT THE LETTER OF THE CORRECT ANSWER IN THE SPACE AT THE RIGHT.*

1) A specialist has been called in to resolve a dispute between two community leaders who have been arguing about the level of service needed within the community. The discussion has been going on for several hours when the specialist arrives, and both people seem to be upset. After calming the two down and getting each of them to agree on a statement of the problem, the specialist should ask each person to

1. _____

A. summarize his or her argument in three main points
B. explain why he or she became so upset
C. clearly state, in objective terms, the position of the other in a form that meets with the other's approval
D. identify the best alternative outcome, other than their presumed ideal

2) In evaluation the impact of a public outreach campaign, the _____ model can be used early in he campaign to address first impressions.

2. _____

A. exposure or advertising
B. expert interview
C. impact monitoring or process
D. experimental or quasi-experimental

3) When trying to motivate an older population to take action on a community problem, it is helpful to remember that older people

3. _____

A. are more self-reliant in their decision-making than other members of the same family
B. often need more time to decide than younger people
C. are more likely than younger people to view community problems self-referentially
D. tend to take a pragmatic, rather than philosophical, view of life

4) The method of group or community decision-making that is normally most time-consuming is

4. _____

A. majority opinion
B. consensus
C. expert opinion
D. authority rule

5) A local adult protective services agency has identified one of the goals of its recent public outreach campaign to be the mobilization of activists. The campaign should probably

A. target neutral audiences
B. home in on supporters
C. stick to purely factual information
D. try to persuade community fence-sitters

5. _____

6) Research of Native American youths' perceptions of family concerns for their well-being has generally found that these youths

A. have a high degree of uncertainty about their families' feelings toward them
B. believe their families don't care about them
C. believe that their mothers care a great deal about them, but their fathers don't
D. believe their families care a great deal about them

6. _____

7) A domestic violence specialist is developing a new outreach program for the local community. The specialist has defined the target problem, set program goals, and planned the actions that will take place as a result of the program. Most likely, the next step will be to

A. evaluate the resources available to achieve program goals
B. define and sequence the steps that will be taken to achieve program goals
C. determine how the program will be evaluated
D. decide how the program will operate

7. _____

8) In the following exchange, what listening skill is evident in the underlined statement?

8. _____

Elder: *I'm so glad to have someone to talk to, someone who really understands my problem.*

Specialist: <u>It is nice to be able to talk to someone who will listen</u>.

Elder: That's for sure.

A. verbatim response
B. paraphrasing
C. advising
D. evaluation

9) Which of the following activities is involved in the specialist's task of mobilizing? 9. _____

A. Meeting individuals in the community with problems and assisting them in finding help
B. Identifying unmet community needs
C. Speaking out against an unjust policy or procedure
D. Developing new services or linking presently available services to meet community needs

10) The preliminary research associated with a public outreach campaign should FIRST be aimed at determining 10. _____

A. the budget
B. the message's ultimate audience
C. what media to use
D. the short-term behavioral goals of the campaign

11) A specialist in a low-income community wants to plan programs that will deal with the influence of unemployment on domestic disturbances. The specialist needs to know not only how many unemployed people are in the community now, but also how many people will be unemployed at any particular time in the future, and how those numbers will vary given certain conditions. Probably the best way to trace employment rates over time and within differing conditions is through the use of 11. _____

A. the critical path method
B. linear programming
C. difference equations
D. the Markov model

12) Generally, public outreach programs—whatever their stated goal—should 12. _____

  I. create a sense of urgency about a problem
  II. decline to identify opponents of the issue or idea
  III. propose concrete, easily understandable solutions
  IV. urge a specific action

A. I only
B. I, III and IV
C. II and III
D. I, II, III and IV

13) Which of the following methods of community needs assessment relies to the greatest degree on existing public records?

A. Social indicators
B. Field study
C. Rates-under treatment
D. Key informant

14) During an interview with a Native American client, a specialist is careful to maintain close and nearly constant eye contact. The client is most likely to interpret this as

A. a show of high concern
B. a sign of disrespect
C. an uncomfortable assumption of intimacy
D. an attempt to intimidate

15) The best strategy for addressing an audience that is known to be captive, or even hostile, is to

A. refer to experiences in common
B. flatter the audience
C. joke about things in or near the audience
D. plead for fairness

16) Integrative conflict resolution is characterized by

A. an overriding concern to maximize joint outcomes
B. one side's interests opposing the other's
C. a fixed and limited amount of resources to be divided, so that the more one group gets, the less another gets
D. manipulation and withholding information as negotiation strategies

17) A specialist wants to learn how to interact with the members of a largely Latino community in a more culturally sensitive way. Which of the following is NOT a guideline for interacting with members of a Latino community?

A. Efforts to foster independence and self-reliance may be interpreted by many Latinos as a lack of concern for others.
B. Efforts to deal one-on-one with an adolescent client may serve to alienate the parents, especially the mother.
C. A nonverbal gesture such as lowering the eyes is interpreted by many Latinos as a sign of respect and deference to authority.
D. In much of Latino culture, the locus of control for problems tends to be much more external than internal.

18) Each of the following is an supporting assumption of community organization, EXCEPT

A. democracy requires cooperative participation
B. in order for communities to change, it is necessary for each individual in the community to be willing to change
C. communities often need help with organization and planning
D. holistic approaches work better than fragmented or ad-hoc programs

18. _____

19) Helping professionals often have difficulty to bring community resources together to fulfill unmet community needs. Which of the following is NOT usually a reason for this?

A. Some community groups resist assistance when it is offered.
B. Few community groups make their needs known.
C. Community resources frequently change the type of services they offer.
D. Often, community resources prefer to work alone

19. _____

20) When dealing with groups or populations of elderly clients, specialists should be mindful that about _____ of the nation's elderly suffer from mental health problems.

A. a tenth
B. a quarter
C. a third
D. half

20. _____

21) In an African American community, a specialist from another culture should recognize that church participation, for most African Americans, is viewed as a

A. method for maintaining control and communicating competency
B. way of depersonalizing problems or troubles
C. way to divert attention away from problems
D. means of cathartic emotional release

21. _____

22) Adult protective service programs supported by state statutes protect elderly people from abuse and neglect under the doctrine of

A. parens patriae
B. habeas corpus
C. in loco parentis
D. volenti non fit injuria

22. _____

23)	In terms of public outreach, which of the following statements about an audience is NOT generally true?

23. _____

A.	The more heterogeneous the audience, the more necessary it will be to use specific examples and appeals to certain types of people
B.	The smaller the audience, the more likely that its members will share assumptions and values
C.	When the speaker does not know the status of an audience, it is best to assume that they are captive rather than voluntary
D.	The larger an audience, the more formal a presentation is likely to be

24)	A specialist often spends time in the places frequented by community residents. She listens carefully to what residents seem most concerned about, and engages many in conversations, asking them how they see the problems in the community. During these conversations, she makes mental notes about whether the statements of the problems are the same things that are mentioned in their conversations. From these conversations, the worker determines what she thinks the unmet needs of the community are. Which of the key issues in identifying unmet needs has the worker neglected to address?

24. _____

A.	The different points of view regarding the issues, and whether there is any common ground.
B.	Whether the stated problems and the conversations with community residents reflect the same concerns.
C.	How community residents define the issues.
D.	What the residents talk about with one another in a community.

25)	Which of the following political styles should be used to promote an issue that could become controversial if it is perceived to involve major reforms?

25. _____

A.	High-conflict, polarized
B.	High-conflict, consensual
C.	Moderate conflict, compromise-oriented
D.	Low-conflict, technical

KEY (CORRECT ANSWERS)

1. C
2. A
3. B
4. B
5. B

6. D
7. A
8. B
9. D
10. B

11. D
12. B
13. A
14. B
15. A

16. A
17. D
18. B
19. C
20. B

21. D
22. A
23. A
24. A
25. D

EXAMINATION SECTION
TEST 1

DIRECTIONS: Each question or incomplete statement is followed by several suggested answers or completions. Select the one that BEST answers the question or completes the statement. *PRINT THE LETTER OF THE CORRECT ANSWER IN THE SPACE AT THE RIGHT.*

1. In public agencies, communications should be based PRIMARILY on a
    A. two-way flow from the top down and from the bottom up, most of which should be given in writing to avoid ambiguity
    B. multidirection flow among all levels and with outside persons
    C. rapid, internal one-way flow from the top down
    D. two-way flow of information, most of which should be given orally for purposes of clarity

2. In some organizations, changes in policy or procedures are often communicated by word of mouth from supervisors to employees with no prior discussion or exchange of viewpoints with employees.
This procedure often produces employee dissatisfaction CHIEFLY because
    A. information is mostly unusable since a considerable amount of time is required to transmit information
    B. lower-level supervisors tend to be excessively concerned with minor details
    C. management has failed to seek employees' advice before making changes
    D. valuable staff time is lost between decision-making and the implementation of decisions

3. For good letter writing, you should try to visualize the person to whom you are writing, especially if you know him.
Of the following rules, it is LEAST helpful in such visualization to think of
    A. the person's likes and dislikes, his concerns, and his needs
    B. what you would be likely to say if speaking in person
    C. what you would expect to be asked if speaking in person
    D. your official position in order to be certain that your words are proper

4. One approach to good informal letter writing is to make letters sound conversational.
All of the following practices will usually help to do this EXCEPT:
    A. If possible, use a style which is similar to the style used when speaking

        B. Substitute phrases for single words (e.g., *at the present time* for *now*)
        C. Use contractions of words (e.g., *you're* for *you are*)
        D. Use ordinary vocabulary when possible

5. All of the following rules will aid in producing clarity in report-writing EXCEPT:
    A. Give specific details or examples, if possible
    B. Keep related words close together in each sentence
    C. Present information in sequential order
    D. Put several thoughts or ideas in each paragraph

6. The one of the following statements about public relations which is MOST accurate is that
    A. in the long run, appearance gains better results than performance
    B. objectivity is decreased if outside public relations consultants are employed
    C. public relations is the responsibility of every employee
    D. public relations should be based on a formal publicity program

7. The form of communication which is usually considered to be MOST personally directed to the intended recipient is the
    A. brochure   B. film   C. letter   D. radio

8. In general, a document that presents an organization's views or opinions on a particular topic is MOST accurately known as a
    A. tear sheet   B. position paper
    C. flyer   D. journal

9. Assume that you have been asked to speak before an organization of persons who oppose a newly announced program in which you are involved. You feel tense about talking to this group.
Which of the following rules generally would be MOST useful in gaining rapport when speaking before the audience?
    A. Impress them with your experience
    B. Stress all areas of disagreement
    C. Talk to the group as to one person
    D. Use formal grammar and language

10. An organization must have an effective public relations program since, at its best, public relations is a bridge to change.
All of the following statements about communication and human behavior have validity EXCEPT:
    A. People are more likely to talk about controversial matters with like-minded people than with those holding other views

B. The earlier an experience, the more powerful its effect since it influences how later experiences will be interpreted
C. In periods of social tension, official sources gain increased believability
D. Those who are already interested in a topic are the ones who are most open to receive new communications about it

11. An employee should be encouraged to talk easily and frankly when he is dealing with his supervisor.
In order to encourage such free communication, it would be MOST appropriate for a supervisor to behave in a(n)
    A. sincere manner; assure the employee that you will deal with him honestly and openly
    B. official manner; you are a supervisor and must always act formally with subordinates
    C. investigative manner; you must probe and question to get to a basis of trust
    D. unemotional manner; the employee's emotions and background should play no part in your dealings with him

12. Research findings show that an increase in free communication within an agency GENERALLY results in which one of the following?
    A. Improved morale and productivity
    B. Increased promotional opportunities
    C. An increase in authority
    D. A spirit of honesty

13. Assume that you are a supervisor and your superiors have given you a new-type procedure to be followed.
Before passing this information on to your subordinates, the one of the following actions that you should take FIRST is to
    A. ask your superiors to send out a memorandum to the entire staff
    B. clarify the procedure in your own mind
    C. set up a training course to provide instruction on the new procedure
    D. write a memorandum to your subordinates

14. Communication is necessary for an organization to be effective.
The one of the following which is LEAST important for most communication systems is that
    A. messages are sent quickly and directly to the person who needs them to operate
    B. information should be conveyed understandably and accurately
    C. the method used to transmit information should be kept secret so that security can be maintained
    D. senders of messages must know how their messages are received and acted upon

15. Which one of the following is the CHIEF advantage of listening willingly to subordinates and encouraging them to talk freely and honestly?
It
    A. reveals to supervisors the degree to which ideas that are passed down are accepted by subordinates
    B. reduces the participation of subordinates in the operation of the department
    C. encourages subordinates to try for promotion
    D. enables supervisors to learn more readily what the *grapevine* is saying

16. A supervisor may be informed through either oral or written reports.
Which one of the following is an ADVANTAGE of using oral reports?
    A. There is no need for a formal record of the report.
    B. An exact duplicate of the report is not easily transmitted to others.
    C. A good oral report requires little time for preparation.
    D. An oral report involves two-way communication between a subordinate and his supervisor.

17. Of the following, the MOST important reason why supervisors should communicate effectively with the public is to
    A. improve the public's understanding of information that is important for them to know
    B. establish a friendly relationship
    C. obtain information about the kinds of people who come to the agency
    D. convince the public that services are adequate

18. Supervisors should generally NOT use phrases like *too hard*, *too easy*, and *a lot* PRINCIPALLY because such phrases
    A. may be offensive to some minority groups
    B. are too informal
    C. mean different things to different people
    D. are difficult to remember

19. The ability to communicate clearly and concisely is an important element in effective leadership.
Which of the following statements about oral and written communication is GENERALLY true?
    A. Oral communication is more time-consuming.
    B. Written communication is more likely to be misinterpreted.
    C. Oral communication is useful only in emergencies.
    D. Written communication is useful mainly when giving information to fewer than twenty people.

20. Rumors can often have harmful and disruptive effects on an organization.
    Which one of the following is the BEST way to prevent rumors from becoming a problem?
    A. Refuse to act on rumors, thereby making them less believable.
    B. Increase the amount of information passed along by the *grapevine*.
    C. Distribute as much factual information as possible.
    D. Provide training in report writing.

21. Suppose that a subordinate asks you about a rumor he has heard. The rumor deals with a subject which your superiors consider *confidential*.
    Which of the following BEST describes how you should answer the subordinate?
    Tell
    A. the subordinate that you don't make the rules and that he should speak to higher ranking officials
    B. the subordinate that you will ask your superior for information
    C. him only that you cannot comment on the matter
    D. him the rumor is not true

22. Supervisors often find it difficult to *get their message across* when instructing newly appointed employees in their various duties.
    The MAIN reason for this is generally that the
    A. duties of the employees have increased
    B. supervisor is often so expert in his area that he fails to see it from the learner's point of view
    C. supervisor adapts his instruction to the slowest learner in the group
    D. new employees are younger, less concerned with job security and more interested in fringe benefits

23. Assume that you are discussing a job problem with an employee under your supervision. During the discussion, you see that the man's eyes are turning away from you and that he is not paying attention.
    In order to get the man's attention, you should FIRST
    A. ask him to look you in the eye
    B. talk to him about sports
    C. tell him he is being very rude
    D. change your tone of voice

24. As a supervisor, you may find it necessary to conduct meetings with your subordinates.
    Of the following, which would be MOST helpful in assuring that a meeting accomplishes the purpose for which it was called?
    A. Give notice of the conclusions you would like to reach at the start of the meeting.
    B. Delay the start of the meeting until everyone is present.

C. Write down points to be discussed in proper sequence.
D. Make sure everyone is clear on whatever conclusions have been reached and on what must be done after the meeting.

25. Every supervisor will occasionally be called upon to deliver a reprimand to a subordinate. If done properly, this can greatly help an employee improve his performance. Which one of the following is NOT a good practice to follow when giving a reprimand?
    A. Maintain your composure and temper.
    B. Reprimand a subordinate in the presence of other employees so they can learn the same lesson.
    C. Try to understand why the employee was not able to perform satisfactorily.
    D. Let your knowledge of the man involved determine the exact nature of the reprimand.

KEY (CORRECT ANSWERS)

1. C
2. B
3. D
4. B
5. D

6. C
7. C
8. B
9. C
10. C

11. A
12. A
13. B
14. C
15. A

16. D
17. A
18. C
19. B
20. C

21. B
22. B
23. D
24. D
25. B

TEST 2

DIRECTIONS: Each question or incomplete statement is followed by several suggested answers or completions. Select the one that BEST answers the question or completes the statement. *PRINT THE LETTER OF THE CORRECT ANSWER IN THE SPACE AT THE RIGHT.*

1. Usually one thinks of communication as a single step, essentially that of transmitting an idea.
   Actually, however, this is only part of a total process, the FIRST step of which should be
   A. the prompt dissemination of the idea to those who may be affected by it
   B. motivating those affected to take the required action
   C. clarifying the idea in one's own mind
   D. deciding to whom the idea is to be communicated

2. Research studies on patterns of informal communication have concluded that most individuals in a group tend to be passive recipients of news, while a few make it their business to spread it around in an organization.
   With this conclusion in mind, it would be MOST correct for the supervisor to attempt to identify these few individuals and
   A. give them the complete facts on important matters in advance of others
   B. inform the other subordinates of the identy of these few individuals so that their influence may be minimized
   C. keep them straight on the facts on important matters
   D. warn them to cease passing along any information to others

3. The one of the following which is the PRINCIPAL advantage of making an oral report is that it
   A. affords an immediate opportunity for two-way communication between the subordinate and superior
   B. is an easy method for the superior to use in transmitting information to others of equal rank
   C. saves the time of all concerned
   D. permits more precise pinpointing of praise or blame by means of follow-up questions by the superior

4. An agency may sometimes undertake a public relations program of a defensive nature.
   With reference to the use of defensive public relations, it would be MOST correct to state that it
   A. is bound to be ineffective since defensive statements, even though supported by factual data, can never hope to even partly overcome the effects of prior unfavorable attacks

B. proves that the agency has failed to establish good relationships with newspapers, radio stations, or other means of publicity
C. shows that the upper echelons of the agency have failed to develop sound public relations procedures and techniques
D. is sometimes required to aid morale by protecting the agency from unjustified criticism and misunderstanding of policies or procedures

5. Of the following factors which contribute to possible undesirable public attitudes towards an agency, the one which is MOST susceptible to being changed by the efforts of the individual employee in an organization is that
   A. enforcement of unpopular regulations has offended many individuals
   B. the organization itself has an unsatisfactory reputation
   C. the public is not interested in agency matters
   D. there are many errors in judgment committed by individual subordinates

6. It is not enough for an agency's services to be of a high quality; attention must also be given to the acceptability of these services to the general public.
   This statement is GENERALLY
   A. *false*; a superior quality of service automatically wins public support
   B. *true*; the agency cannot generally progress beyond the understanding and support of the public
   C. *false*; the acceptance by the public of agency services determines their quality
   D. *true*; the agency is generally unable to engage in any effective enforcement activity without public support

7. Sustained agency participation in a program sponsored by a community organization is MOST justified when
   A. the achievement of agency objectives in some area depends partly on the activity of this organization
   B. the community organization is attempting to widen the base of participation in all community affairs
   C. the agency is uncertain as to what the community wants
   D. there is an obvious lack of good leadership in a newly formed community organization

8. Of the following, the LEAST likely way in which a records system may serve a supervisor is in
   A. developing a sympathetic and cooperative public attitude toward the agency
   B. improving the quality of supervision by permitting a check on the accomplishment of subordinates
   C. permit a precise prediction of the exact incidences in specific categories for the following year
   D. helping to take the guesswork out of the distribution of the agency

9. Assuming that the *grapevine* in any organization is virtually indestructible, the one of the following which it is MOST important for management to understand is:
   A. What is being spread by means of the *grapevine* and the reason for spreading it
   B. What is being spread by means of the *grapevine* and how it is being spread
   C. Who is involved in spreading the information that is on the *grapevine*
   D. Why those who are involved in spreading the information are doing so

10. When the supervisor writes a report concerning an investigation to which he has been assigned, it should be LEAST intended to provide
    A. a permanent official record of relevant information gathered
    B. a summary of case findings limited to facts which tend to indicate the guilt of a suspect
    C. a statement of the facts on which higher authorities may base a corrective or disciplinary action
    D. other investigators with information so that they may continue with other phases of the investigation

11. In survey work, questionnaires rather than interviews are sometimes used.
    The one of the following which is a DISADVANTAGE of the questionnaire method as compared with the interview is the
    A. difficulty of accurately interpreting the results
    B. problem of maintaining anonymity of the participant
    C. fact that it is relatively uneconomical
    D. requirement of special training for the distribution of questionnaires

12. In his contacts with the public, an employee should attempt to create a good climate of support for his agency.
    This statement is GENERALLY
    A. *false*; such attempts are clearly beyond the scope of his responsibility
    B. *true*; employees of an agency who come in contact with the public have the opportunity to affect public relations
    C. *false*; such activity should be restricted to supervisors trained in public relations techniques
    D. *true*; the future expansion of the agency depends to a great extent on continued public support of the agency

13. The repeated use by a supervisor of a call for volunteers to get a job done is objectionable MAINLY because it
    A. may create a feeling of animosity between the volunteers and the non-volunteers
    B. may indicate that the supervisor is avoiding responsibility for making assignments which will be most productive

C. is an indication that the supervisor is not familiar with the individual capabilities of his men
D. is unfair to men who, for valid reasons, do not, or cannot volunteer

14. Of the following statements concerning subordinates' expressions to a supervisor of their opinions and feelings concerning work situations, the one which is MOST correct is that
    A. by listening and responding to such expressions the supervisor encourages the development of complaints
    B. the lack of such expressions should indicate to the supervisor that there is a high level of job satisfaction
    C. the more the supervisor listens to and responds to such expressions, the more he demonstrates lack of supervisory ability
    D. by listening and responding to such expressions, the supervisor will enable many subordinates to understand and solve their own problems on the job

15. In attempting to motivate employees, rewards are considered preferable to punishment PRIMARILY because
    A. punishment seldom has any effect on human behavior
    B. punishment usually results in decreased production
    C. supervisors find it difficult to punish
    D. rewards are more likely to result in willing cooperation

16. In an attempt to combat the low morale in his organization, a high-level supervisor publicized an *open-door* policy to allow employees who wished to do so to come to him with their complaints.
    Which of the following is LEAST likely to account for the fact that no employee came in with a complaint?
    A. Employees are generally reluctant to go over the heads of their immediate supervisors.
    B. The employees did not feel that management would help them.
    C. The low morale was not due to complaints associated with the job.
    D. The employees felt that they had more to lose than to gain.

17. It is MOST desirable to use written instructions rather than oral instructions for a particular job when
    A. a mistake on the job will not be serious
    B. the job can be completed in a short time
    C. there is no need to explain the job minutely
    D. the job involves many details

18. If you receive a telephone call regarding a matter which   18.____
    your office does not handle, you should FIRST
    A. give the caller the telephone number of the proper
       office so that he can dial again
    B. offer to transfer the caller to the proper office
    C. suggest that the caller re-dial since he probably
       dialed incorrectly
    D. tell the caller he has reached the wrong office and
       then hang up

19. When you answer the telephone, the MOST important reason   19.____
    for identifying yourself and your organization is to
    A. give the caller time to collect his or her thoughts
    B. impress the caller with your courtesy
    C. inform the caller that he or she has reached the
       right number
    D. set a business-like tone at the beginning of the
       conversation

20. As soon as you pick up the phone, a very angry caller   20.____
    begins immediately to complain about city agencies and
    red tape. He says that he has been shifted to two or
    three different offices. It turns out that he is seeking
    information which is not immediately available to you.
    You believe you know, however, where it can be found.
    Which of the following actions is the BEST one for you
    to take?
    A. To eliminate all confusion, suggest that the caller
       write the agency stating explicitly what he wants.
    B. Apologize by telling the caller how busy city
       agencies now are, but also tell him directly that
       you do not have the information he needs.
    C. Ask for the caller's telephone number and assure
       him you will call back after you have checked further.
    D. Give the caller the name and telephone number of the
       person who might be able to help, but explain that
       you are not positive he will get results.

21. Which of the following approaches usually provides the   21.____
    BEST communication in the objectives and values of a
    new program which is to be introduced?
    A. A general written description of the program by the
       program manager for review by those who share
       responsibility
    B. An effective verbal presentation by the program
       manager to those affected
    C. Development of the plan and operational approach in
       carrying out the program by the program manager
       assisted by his key subordinates
    D. Development of the plan by the program manager's
       supervisor

22. What is the BEST approach for introducing change?
    A
    A. combination of written and also verbal communication to all personnel affected by the change
    B. general bulletin to all personnel
    C. meeting pointing out all the values of the new approach
    D. written directive to key personnel

23. Of the following, committees are BEST used for
    A. advising the head of the organization
    B. improving functional work
    C. making executive decisions
    D. making specific planning decisions

24. An effective discussion leader is one who
    A. announces the problem and his preconceived solution at the start of the discussion
    B. guides and directs the discussion according to pre-arranged outline
    C. interrupts or corrects confused participants to save time
    D. permits anyone to say anything at anytime

25. The human relations movement in management theory is BASICALLY concerned with
    A. counteracting employee unrest
    B. eliminating the *time and motion* man
    C. interrelationships among individuals in organizations
    D. the psychology of the worker

KEY (CORRECT ANSWERS)

1. C
2. C
3. A
4. D
5. D

6. B
7. A
8. C
9. A
10. B

11. A
12. B
13. B
14. D
15. D

16. C
17. D
18. B
19. C
20. C

21. C
22. A
23. A
24. B
25. C

EXAMINATION SECTION
TEST 1

DIRECTIONS: Each question or incomplete statement is followed by several suggested answers or completions. Select the one that BEST answers the question or completes the statement. *PRINT THE LETTER OF THE CORRECT ANSWER IN THE SPACE AT THE RIGHT.*

1. Which of the following is the acceptable format for typing the date line?
   A. 12/2/96
   B. December 2, 1996
   C. December 2nd, 1996
   D. Dec. 2 1996

1.___

2. When typing a letter, which of the following is INACCURATE?
   A. If the letter is to be more than one page long, subsequent sheets should be blank, but should match the letterhead sheet in size, color, weight, and texture.
   B. Long quoted material must be centered and single-spaced internally.
   C. Quotation marks must be used when there is long quoted material.
   D. Double spacing is used above and below tables and long quotations to set them off from the rest of the material.

2.___

3. Which of the following is INACCURATE?
   A. When an addressee's title in an inside address would overrun the center of a page, it's best to carry part of the title over to another line and to indent it by two spaces.
   B. It is permissible to use ordinal numbers in an inside address.
   C. In addresses involving street numbers under three, the number is written out in full.
   D. In the inside address, suite, apartment or room numbers should be placed on the line after the street address.

3.___

4. All of the following are common styles of business letters EXCEPT
   A. simplified
   B. block
   C. direct
   D. executive

4.___

5. Please select the two choices below that correctly represent how a continuation sheet heading may be typed.
   I. Page 2
      Mr. Alan Post
      June 25, 1996
   II. Page 2
      Mr. Alan Post
      6-25-96
   III. Mr. Alan Post   -2-
      June 25, 1996
   IV. Mr. Alan Post   -2-
      6-25-96

5.___

The CORRECT answer is:
A. I,II   B. II,III   C. I,III   D. II,IV

6. Which of the following is INCORRECT? 6.___
   It is
   A. permissible to abbreviate honorifics in the inside address
   B. permissible to abbreviate company or organizational names, departmental designations, or organizational titles in the inside address
   C. permissible to use abbreviations in the inside address if they have been used on the printed letterhead and form part of the official company name
   D. sometimes permissible to omit the colon after the salutation

7. Which of the following is INCORRECT? 7.___
   A. The subject line of a letter gives the main idea of the message as succinctly as possible.
   B. If a letter contains an enclosure, there should be a notation indicating this.
   C. Important enclosures ought to be listed numerically and described.
   D. An enclosure notation should be typed flush with the right margin.

8. Which of the following is INACCURATE about inside addresses? 8.___
   A. An intraoffice or intracompany mail stop number such as DA 3C 61B is put after the organization or company name with at least two spaces intervening.
   B. Words such as *Avenue* should not be abbreviated.
   C. With the exception of runovers, the inside address should not be more than five full lines.
   D. The inside address includes the recipient's courtesy or honorific title and his or her full name on line one; the recipient's title on the next line; the recipient's official organizational affiliation on the next line; the street address on the penultimate line; and the city, state, and zip code on the last line.

9. Which of the following is an INCORRECT example of how to copy recipients when using copy notation? 9.___
   A. cc: Martin A. Sheen
   B. cc: Ms. Connors
       Ms. Grogan
       Ms. Reynolds
   C. CC: Martin A. Sheen
   D. cc: Mr. Right
       Mr. Wrong
       Mr. Perfect

10. When typing a memo, all of the following are true EXCEPT   10.___
    A. it is permissible to use an abbreviation like 1/1/91
    B. the subject line should be underlined
    C. titles such as *Mr.* or *Dr.* are usually not used on
       the *To* line
    D. unless the memo is very short, paragraphs should be
       single-spaced and double spacing should be used to
       separate the paragraphs from each other

11. When typing a letter, which of the following is INACCURATE?   11.___
    A. Paragraphs in business letters are usually single-
       spaced, with double spacing separating them from
       each other.
    B. Margin settings used on subsequent sheets should
       match those used on the letterhead sheet.
    C. If the message contains an enumerated list, it is
       best to block and center the listed material by five
       or six more spaces, right and left.
    D. A quotation of more than three typed lines must be
       single-spaced and centered on the page.

12. A letter that is to be signed by Hazel Alice Putney, but   12.___
    written by Mary Jane Roberts, and typed by Alice Carol
    Bell would CORRECTLY bear the following set of initials:
    A. HAP:MJR:acb   B. HAP:MJR:ab
    C. HAP:mjr:acb   D. HAP:mjr:ab

13. Which of the following is INCORRECT?   13.___
    A. My dear Dr. Jones:
    B. Dear Accounting Department:
    C. Dear Dr. Jones:
    D. Dear Mr. Al Lee, Esq.:

14. Which of the following is INCORRECT?   14.___
    A. Bcc stands for blind copy or blind courtesy copy.
    B. When a blind copy is used, the notation bcc appears
       only on the original.
    C. When a blind copy is used, the notation may appear
       in the top left corner of the letterhead sheet.
    D. If following a letter style that uses indented
       paragraphs, the postscript should be indented in
       exactly the same manner.

15. All of the following are true of the complimentary close   15.___
    EXCEPT
    A. it is typed two lines beneath the last line of the
       message
    B. when using a minimal punctuation system, you may omit
       the comma in the complimentary close if you have
       used a colon in the salutation
    C. where the complimentary close is placed may vary
    D. the first word of the complimentary close is
       capitalized

16. When typing a letter, which of the following is INACCURATE?
    A. Tables should be centered.
    B. If the letter is to be more than one page long, at least three lines of the message itself should be carried over.
    C. The message begins two lines below the salutation in almost all letter styles.
    D. Triple spacing should be used above and below lists to set them off from the rest of the letter.

17. Which one of the following is INCORRECT?
    A. When used, special mailing instructions should be indicated on both the envelope and the letter itself.
    B. Depending upon the length of the message and the available space, special mailing instructions are usually typed flush left, about four spaces below the date line and about two lines above the first line of the inside address.
    C. Certification, registration, special delivery, and overseas air mail are all considered special mailing instructions.
    D. Special mailing instructions should not be typed in capital letters.

18. Which of the following is INCORRECT?
    A. When a letter is intended to be personal or confidential, these instructions are typewritten in capital letters on the envelope and on the letter itself.
    B. When a letter is intended to be personal or confidential, these instructions are typewritten in capital letters on the envelope, but not on the letter.
    C. A letter marked PERSONAL is an eyes-only communication for the recipient.
    D. A letter marked CONFIDENTIAL means that the recipient and any other authorized person may open and read it.

19. All of the following are true in regard to copy notation EXCEPT
    A. when included in a letter, a copy notation should be typed flush with the left margin, two lines below the signature block or two lines below any preceding notation
    B. copy notation should appear after writer/typist initials and/or enclosure notations, if these are used
    C. the copy recipient's full name and address should be indicated
    D. if more than one individual is to be copied, recipients should be listed in alphabetical order according to full name or initials

20. When addressing envelopes, which of the following is INACCURATE?
    A. When both street address and box number are used, the destination of the letter should be placed on the line just above the city, state, and zip code line.
    B. Special mailing instructions are typed in capital letters below the postage.
    C. Special handling instructions should be typed in capital letters and underlined.
    D. The address should be single-spaced.

21. All of the following should be capitalized EXCEPT the
    A. first word of a direct quotation
    B. first word in the continuation of a split, single-sentence quotation
    C. names of organizations
    D. names of places and geographic districts, regions, divisions, and locales

22. All of the following are true about capitalization EXCEPT
    A. words indicating direction and regions are capitalized
    B. the names of rivers, seas, lakes, mountains, and oceans are capitalized
    C. the names of nationalities, tribes, languages, and races are capitalized
    D. civil, military, corporate, royal and noble, honorary, and religious titles are capitalized when they precede a name

23. All of the following are true about capitalization EXCEPT
    A. key words in the titles of musical, dramatic, artistic, and literary works are capitalized as are the first and last words
    B. the first word of the salutation and of the complimentary close of a letter is capitalized
    C. abbreviations and acronyms are not capitalized
    D. the days of the week, months of the year, holidays, and holy days are capitalized

24. All of the following are true EXCEPT
    A. an apostrophe indicates the omission of letters in contractions
    B. an apostrophe indicates the possessive case of singular and plural nouns
    C. an apostrophe should not be used to indicate the omission of figures in dates
    D. ellipses are used to indicate the omission of words or sentences within quoted material

25. All of the following are true EXCEPT
    A. brackets may be used to enclose words or passages in quotations to indicate the insertion of material written by someone other than the original writer
    B. brackets may be used to enclose material that is inserted within material already in parentheses
    C. a dash, rather than a colon, should be used to introduce a list
    D. a colon may be used to introduce a long quotation

26. All of the following are true EXCEPT a(n)
    A. comma may be used to set off short quotations and sayings
    B. apostrophe is often used to represent the word *per*
    C. dash may be used to indicate a sudden change or break in continuity
    D. dash may be used to set apart an emphatic or defining phrase

27. All of the following are true EXCEPT
    A. a hyphen may be used as a substitute for the word *to* between figures or words
    B. parentheses are used to enclose material that is not an essential part of the sentence and that, if not included, would not change its meaning
    C. single quotation marks are used to enclose quotations within quotations
    D. semicolons and colons are put inside closing quotation marks

28. All of the following are true EXCEPT
    A. commas and periods should be put inside closing quotation marks
    B. for dramatic effect, a semicolon may be used instead of a comma to signal longer pauses
    C. a semicolon is used to set off city and state in geographic names
    D. italics are used to represent the titles of magazines and newspapers

29. According to standard rules for typing, two spaces are left after a
    A. closing parenthesis   B. comma
    C. number   D. colon

30. All of the following are true EXCEPT
    A. rounding out large numbers is often acceptable
    B. it is best to use numerical figures to express specific hours, measures, dates, page numbers, coordinates, and addresses
    C. when a sentence begins with a number, it is best to use numerical figures rather than to spell the number out
    D. when two or more numbers appear in one sentence, it is best to spell them out consistently or use numerical figures consistently, regardless of the size of the numbers

31. All of the following are true about word division EXCEPT   31.___
    A. words should not be divided on a single letter
    B. it is acceptable to carry over two-letter endings
    C. the final word in a paragraph should not be divided
    D. words in headings should not be divided

32. All of the following are true of word division EXCEPT   32.___
    A. it is preferable to divide words of three or more
       syllables after the consonant
    B. it is best to avoid breaking words on more than two
       consecutive lines
    C. words should be divided according to pronunciation
    D. two-syllable words are divided at the end of the
       first syllable

33. All of the following are true of word division EXCEPT   33.___
    A. words with short prefixes should be divided after
       the prefix
    B. prefixes and combining forms of more than one
       syllable should be divided after the first syllable
    C. the following word endings are not divided: -gion,
       -gious, -sial, -sion, -tial, -tion, -tious, -ceous,
       -cial, -cient, -cion, -cious, and -geous
    D. words ending in -er should not be divided if the
       division could only occur on the -er form

34. All of the following are true about word division EXCEPT   34.___
    A. words should be divided so that the part of the word
       left at the end of the line will suggest the word
    B. abbreviations should not be divided
    C. the suffixes -able and -ible are usually divided
       instead of being carried over intact to the next line
    D. when the addition of -ed, -est, -er, or a similar
       ending causes the doubling of a final consonant, the
       added consonant is carried over

35. All of the following are true of word division EXCEPT   35.___
    A. words with doubled consonants are usually divided
       between those consonants
    B. it is permissible to divide contractions
    C. words of one syllable should not be split
    D. it is best to try to avoid divisions that add a
       hyphen to an already hyphenated word

36. All of the following are true of word division EXCEPT   36.___
    A. dividing proper names should be avoided wherever
       possible
    B. two consonants, preceded and followed by a vowel,
       are divided after the first consonant
    C. even though two adjoining vowels are sounded separate-
       ly, it is best not to divide between the two vowels
    D. it is best not to divide the month and day when
       typing dates, but the year may be carried over to
       the next line

37. Which of the following four statements are CORRECT?
    It would be acceptable to divide the word
    I. *organization* after the first *a* in the word
    II. *recommend* after the first *m*
    III. *interface* between the *r* and the *f*
    IV. *development* between the *e* and the *l*

    The CORRECT answer is:
    A. I *only*   B. II, III
    C. II *only*   D. I, II, III

38. Which of the following is divided INCORRECTLY?
    A. usu-ally   B. call-ing
    C. pro-blem   D. micro-computer

39. Which of the following is divided INCORRECTLY?
    A. imag-inary   B. commun-ity
    C. manage-able   D. commun-ion

40. Which of the following is divided INCORRECTLY?
    A. spa-ghetti   B. retro-spective
    C. proof-reader   D. fix-ed

41. Which of the following is divided INCORRECTLY?
    A. Mr. Han-rahan   B. control-lable
    C. pro-jectile   D. proj-ect

42. Which of the following is divided INCORRECTLY?
    A. prom-ise   B. han-dling
    C. have-n't   D. pro-duce

43. Which of the following is divided INCORRECTLY?
    A. ship-ped   B. audi-ble
    C. hypo-crite   D. refer-ring

44. Which of the following is divided INCORRECTLY?
    A. particu-lar   B. spac-ious
    C. chang-ing   D. capac-ity

45. There is a critical need to develop the ability to control the mind, especailly the ability to stop repeating negative thoughts. Often, when we must swallow our anger, we are left running an enless tape of thoughts. We can't stop thinking about what the person said and what we should have said in response. To combat this tendency, it is helpful to practice witnessing our thoughts. If we can remain detached from them, we won't fuel them, and they will just run out of gas. As we watch them, we also learn alot about ourselves. The catch here is not to judge them. Judging may lead to selfblaming, blaming others, excuses, rationalizations, and other thoughts that just add fuel. Another technique is is substituting positive thoughts for negative ones.

It is difficult to do this in the "heat of the moment".
With practice, however, its possible to train the mind to
do what we want it to do and to contain what we want it to
contain. A mind is like a garden -- we can weed it, or we
can let it grow wild.
The above paragraph contains a number of typographical
errors.
How many lines in this paragraph contain typographical
errors?
    A. 5   B. 6   C. 8   D. 9

KEY (CORRECT ANSWERS)

1. B	11. D	21. B	31. B	41. A
2. C	12. A	22. A	32. A	42. A
3. D	13. D	23. C	33. B	43. A
4. C	14. B	24. C	34. C	44. B
5. C	15. B	25. C	35. B	45. C
6. B	16. D	26. B	36. C	
7. D	17. D	27. D	37. B	
8. B	18. B	28. C	38. C	
9. D	19. C	29. D	39. B	
10. B	20. C	30. C	40. D	

TEST 2

DIRECTIONS: Each sentence may or may not contain problems in capitalization or punctuation. If there is an error, select the number of the underlined part that must be changed to make the sentence correct. If the sentence has no error, select choice E. <u>No sentence contains more than one error.</u>

1. Is the choice for $\underset{A}{\underline{President}}$ of the company $\underset{B}{\underline{George}}$ $\underset{C}{\underline{Dawson}}$ or Marilyn $\underset{D}{\underline{Kappel?}}$ $\underset{E}{\underline{\text{No error}}}$ 1.___

2. "To tell you the $\underset{A}{\underline{truth,}}$ I was really $\underset{B}{\underline{disappointed\ that}}$ our $\underset{C}{\underline{Fall}}$ percentages did not show more sales $\underset{D}{\underline{growth,}}$" remarked the bookkeeper. $\underset{E}{\underline{\text{No error}}}$ 2.___

3. Bruce gave his $\underset{A}{\underline{Uncle}}$ clear directions to go $\underset{B}{\underline{south}}$ on Maplewood $\underset{C}{\underline{Drive,}}$ turn left at the intersection with Birch Lane, and then proceed for two miles until he reached Columbia $\underset{D}{\underline{County.}}$ $\underset{E}{\underline{\text{No error}}}$ 3.___

4. Janet hopes to transfer to a $\underset{A}{\underline{college}}$ in the $\underset{B}{\underline{east}}$ $\underset{C}{\underline{during}}$ her $\underset{D}{\underline{junior}}$ year. $\underset{E}{\underline{\text{No error}}}$ 4.___

5. The $\underset{A}{\underline{Declaration}}$ $\underset{B}{\underline{of}}$ Independence $\underset{C}{\underline{states\ that}}$ we have the right to the pursuit of $\underset{D}{\underline{Happiness,}}$ but it doesn't guarantee that we'll ever find it. $\underset{E}{\underline{\text{No error}}}$ 5.___

6. We campaigned hard for the $\underset{A}{\underline{mayor,}}$ $\underset{B}{\underline{but}}$ $\underset{C}{\underline{we're}}$ still not sure if he'll win against $\underset{D}{\underline{Senator}}$ Frankovich. $\underset{E}{\underline{\text{No error}}}$ 6.___

7. Mr. $\underset{A}{\underline{Butler's}}$ $\underset{B}{\underline{Ford}}$ was parked right behind $\underset{C}{\underline{our's}}$ on Atlantic $\underset{D}{\underline{Avenue.}}$ $\underset{E}{\underline{\text{No error}}}$ 7.___

8. "I respect your opinion, but I cannot agree with it,"
         A   B   C
    commented my grandmother. No error
                    D   E

9. My friends, of course, were surprised when I did so well
          A   B   C
    on the Math section of the test. No error
           D   E

10. Dr. Vogel and Senator Rydell decided that the meeting
                    A   B
    would be held on February 6, in Ithaca, New York.
                          C   D
    No error
      E

11. "Frank do you understand what we're telling you?" asked
         A   B   C
    the doctor. No error
         D   E

12. When I asked my daughter what she knew about politics she
                   A   B
    claimed she knew nothing. No error
        C   D   E

13. "If you went to my high school, dad, you'd see things
                 A A   B C   D
    differently," snapped Sean. No error
                              E

14. In Carlos' third year of high school, he took geometry,
         A   B B
    psychology, french, and chemistry. No error
     C   D   E

15. "When you enter the building," the guard instructed us,
                         A   B
    "turn left down the long, winding corridor." No error
      C   D   E

16. We hope to spend a weekend in the Catskill Mountains in
                                         A
    the spring, and we'd like to go to Florida in January.
       B   C   D
    No error
      E

17. A clerk in the department of Justice asked Carol and me
      A   B   C
    if we were there on business or just sight-seeing.
                                            D
    No error
      E

18. Jamie joined a cult, Harry's in a rock band, and Carol-Ann   18.___
            A   B
    is studying chinese literature at the University of
              C   D
    Southern California. No error
                            E

19. Parker Flash asked if my band had ever played at the   19.___
                     A
    Purple Turnip a club in Orinoco Hills. No error
    B   C   D   E

20. "The gift of the Magi" is a short story by O'Henry that   20.___
         A   B   C   D
    deals with the sad ironies of life. No error
                                          E

21. Darwin's theory was developed, as a result of his trip to   21.___
        A   B   C
    the Galapagos Islands. No error
                 D   E

22. Is 10 Downing street the address of Sherlock Holmes or the   22.___
            A   B
    British Prime Minister? No error
    C   D   E

23. While President Johnson was in Office, his Great Society   23.___
            A   B   C   D   D
    program passed a great deal of important legislation.

    No error
      E

24. If, as the American Industrial Health Council's study   24.___
       A   B   C
    says, one out of every five cancers today is caused by

    the workplace it is a tragic indictment of what is
                 D
    happening there. No error
                        E

25. According to the Articles of Confederation, Congress   25.___
                              A   B
    could issue money, but it could not prevent States from
                    C   D
    issuing their own money. No error
                               E

26. "I'd really like to know whos going to be shoveling the   26.___
                            A B
    driveway this winter," said Laverne. No error
                 C   D   E

27. According to Carl Jung the Swiss psychologist, playing   27.___
         ───── ────   ─────
           A   B   C
    with fantasy is the key to creativity. No error
                        ───   ────────
                         D   E

28. Don't you find it odd that people would prefer jumping   28.___
       ──
       A
    off the Golden Gate bridge to jumping off other bridges
                        ──────
                          B
    in the area? No error
           ────   ────────
            C   D   E

29. While driving through the South, we saw many of the   29.___
                            ──────
                              A   B
    sites of famous Civil war battles. No error
                         ─── ───────   ────────
                          C   D   E

30. Although I have always valued my Grandmother's china, I 30.___
                                     ─────────── ─────
                                          A   B C
    prefer her collection of South American art. No error
                             ──────────────────   ────────
                                     D   E

KEY (CORRECT ANSWERS)

1. A   11. A   21. C
2. C   12. B   22. B
3. A   13. C   23. B
4. B   14. D   24. D
5. D   15. E   25. D

6. E   16. E   26. B
7. C   17. B   27. A
8. E   18. C   28. B
9. D   19. C   29. C
10. E   20. A   30. A

CLERICAL ABILITIES
EXAMINATION SECTION

TEST 1

DIRECTIONS: Each question or incomplete statement is followed by several suggested answers or completions. Select the one that BEST answers the question or completes the statement. *PRINT THE LETTER OF THE CORRECT ANSWER IN THE SPACE AT THE RIGHT.*

Questions 1 through 4 are to be answered on the basis of the information below:

The most commonly used filing system and the one that is easiest to learn is alphabetical filing. This involves putting records in an A to Z order, according to the letters of the alphabet. The name of a person is filed by using the following order: first, the surname or last name; second, the first name; third, the middle name or initial. For example, *Henry C. Young* is filed under *Y* and thereafter under *Young, Henry C.* The name of a company is filed in the same way. For example, *Long Cabinet Co.* is filed under *L*, while *John T. Long Cabinet Co.* is filed under *L* and thereafter under *Long, John T. Cabinet Co.*

1. The one of the following which lists the names of the persons in the CORRECT alphabetical order is
    A. Mary Carrie, Helen Carrol, James Carson, John Carter
    B. James Carson, Mary Carrie, John Carter, Helen Carrol
    C. Helen Carrol, James Carson, John Carter, Mary Carrie
    D. John Carter, Helen Carrol, Mary Carrie, James Carson

1._____

2. The one of the following which lists the names of the persons in the CORRECT alphabetical order is
    A. Jones, John C.; Jones, John A.; Jones, John P.; Jones, John K.
    B. Jones, John P.; Jones, John K.; Jones, John C.; Jones, John A.
    C. Jones, John A.; Jones, John C.; Jones, John K.; Jones, John P.
    D. Jones, John K.; Jones, John C,; Jones, John A.; Jones, John P.

2._____

3. The one of the following which lists the names of the companies in CORRECT alphabetical order is
    A. Blane Co., Blake Co., Block Co., Blear Co.
    B. Blake Co., Blane Co., Blear Co., Block Co.
    C. Block Co., Blear Co., Blane Co., Blake Co.
    D. Blear Co., Blake Co., Blane Co., Block Co.

3._____

4. You are to return to the file an index card on *Barry C. Wayne Materials and Supplies Co.* Of the following, the CORRECT alphabetical group that you should return the index card to is
    A. A to G   B. H to M   C. N to S   D. T to Z

4._____

Questions 5-10

DIRECTIONS: In each of questions 5 through 10, the names of four people are given. For each question, choose as your answer the one of the four names given which would be filed FIRST according to the usual system of alphabetical filing of names, as described in the following paragraph.

In filing names, you must start with the last name. Names are filed in order of the first letter of the last name, then the second letter, etc. Therefore, BAILY would be filed by BROWN, which would be filed before COLT. A name with fewer letters of the same type comes first; i.e., Smith before Smithe. If the last names are the same, the names are filed alphabetically by the first name. If the first name is an initial, a name with an initial would come before a first name that starts with the same letter as the initial. Therefore, I. BROWN would come before IRA BROWN. Finally, if both last name and first name are the same, the name would be filed alphabetically by the middle name, once again an initial coming before a middle name which starts with the same letter as the initial. If there is no middle name at all, the name would come before those with middle initials or names.

Sample Question:
- A. Lester Daniels
- B. William Dancer
- C. Nathan Danzig
- D. Dan Lester

The last names beginning with D are filed before the last name beginning with L. Since DANIELS, DANCER and DANZIG all begin with the same three letters, you must look at the fourth letter of the last name to determine which name should be filed first. C comes before I or Z, so DANCER is filed before DANIELS or DANZIG. Therefore, the answer to the question is B.

5. A. Scott Biala B. Mary Byala
   C. Martin Baylor D. Francis Bauer

6. A. Howard J. Black B. Howard Black
   C. J. Howard Black D. John H. Black

7. A. Theodora Garth Kingston B. Theadore Barth Kingston
   C. Thomas Kingston D. Thomas T. Kingston

8. A. Paulette Mary Huerta B. Paul M. Huerta
   C. Paulette L. Huerta D. Peter A. Huerta

9. A. Martha Hunt Morgan   B. Martin Hunt Morgan
C. Mary H. Morgan   D. Martine H. Morgan

9._____

10. A. James T. Meerschaum   B. James M. Mershum
C. James F. Mearshaum   D. James N. Meshum

10._____

Questions 11 through 14 are to be answered on the basis of the following information:

You are required to file various documents in file drawers which are labeled according to the following pattern:

DOCUMENTS

MEMOS			LETTERS	
File	Subject		File	Subject
84PM1	(A-L)		84PC1	(A-L)
84PM2	(M-Z)		84PC2	(M-Z)

REPORTS			INQUIRIES	
File	Subject		File	Subject
84PR1	(A-L)		84PQ1	(A-L)
84PR2	(M-Z)		84PQ2	(M-Z)

11. A letter dealing with a burglary should be filed in the drawer labeled
    A. 84PM1   B. 84PC1   C. 84PR1   D. 84PQ2

11._____

12. A report on Statistics should be found in the drawer labeled
    A. 84PM1   B. 84PC2   C. 84PR2   D. 84PQ2

12._____

13. An inquiry is received about parade permit procedures. It should be filed in the drawer labeled
    A. 84PM2   B. 84PC1   C. 84PR1   D. 84PQ2

13._____

14. A police officer has a question about a robbery report you filed. You should pull this file from the drawer labeled
    A. 84PM1   B. 84PM2   C. 84PR1   D. 84PR2

14._____

Questions 15-22

DIRECTIONS: Each of questions 15 through 22 consist of four or six numbered names. For each question, choose the option which indicates the order in which the names should be filed in accordance with the following filing instructions:

- File alphabetically according to last name, then first name, then middle initial
- File according to each successive letter within a name
- When comparing two names in which the letters in the longer name are identical to the corresponding letters in the shorter name, the shorter name is filed first
- When the last names are the same, initials are always filed before names beginning with the same letter

15. I.   Ralph Robinson   II. Alfred Ross
    III. Luis Robles   IV. James Roberts

    The CORRECT filing sequence for the above names should be
    A. IV, II, I, III   B. I, IV, III, II
    C. III, IV, I, II   D. IV, I, III, II

16. I.   Irwin Goodwin   II. Inez Gonzalez
    III. Irene Goodman   IV. Ira S. Goodwin
    V.   Ruth I. Goldstein   VI. M.B. Goodman

    The CORRECT filing sequence for the above names should be
    A. V, II, I, IV, III, VI   B. V, II, VI, III, IV, I
    C. V, II, III, VI, IV, I   D. V, II, III, VI, I, IV

17. I.   George Allan   II. Gregory Allen
    III. Gary Allen   IV. George Allen

    The CORRECT filing sequence for the above names should be
    A. IV, III, I, II   B. I, IV, II, III
    C. III, IV, I, II   D. I, III, IV, II

18. I.   Simon Kauffman   II. Leo Kaufman
    III. Robert Kaufmann   IV. Paul Kauffmann

    The CORRECT filing sequence for the above names should be
    A. I, IV, II, III   B. II, IV, III, I
    C. III, II, IV, I   D. I, II, III, IV

5 (#1)

19. I. Roberta Williams   II. Robin Wilson
    III. Roberta Wilson   IV. Robin Williams

    The CORRECT filing sequence for the above names should be
    A. III, II, IV, I
    B. I, IV, III, II
    C. I, II, III, IV
    D. III, I, II, IV

20. I. Lawrence Shultz   II. Albert Schultz
    III. Theodore Schwartz   IV. Thomas Schwarz
    V. Alvin Schultz   VI. Leonard Shultz

    The CORRECT filing sequence for the above names should be
    A. II, V, III, IV, I, VI
    B. IV, III, V, I, II, VI
    C. II, V, I, VI, III, IV
    D. I, VI, II, V, III, IV

21. I. McArdle   II. Mayer
    III. Maletz   IV. McNiff
    V. Meyer   VI. MacMahon

    The CORRECT filing sequence for the above names should be
    A. I, IV, VI, III, II, V
    B. II, I, IV, VI, III, V
    C. VI, III, II, I, IV, V
    D. VI, III, II, V, I, IV

22. I. Jack E. Johnson   II. R.H. Jackson
    III. Bertha Jackson   IV. J.T. Johnson
    V. Ann Johns   VI. John Jacobs

    The CORRECT filing sequence for the above names should be
    A. II, III, VI, V, IV, I
    B. III, II, VI, V, IV, I
    C. VI, II, III, I, V, IV
    D. III, II, VI, IV, V, I

Questions 23-30

DIRECTIONS: The code table below shows 10 letters with matching numbers. For each question, there are three sets of letters. Each set of letters is followed by a set of numbers which may or may not match their correct letter according to the code table. For each question, check all three sets of letters and numbers and mark your answer:

      A. if no pairs are correctly matched
      B. if only one pair is correctly matched
      C. if only two pairs are correctly matched
      D. if all three pairs are correctly matched

CODE TABLE

T	M	V	D	S	P	R	G	B	H
1	2	3	4	5	6	7	8	9	0

Sample Question:
    TMVDSP – 123456
    RGBHTM – 789011
    DSPRGB – 256789

In the sample question above, the first set of numbers correctly matches its set of letters. But the second and third pairs contain mistakes. In the second pair, M is incorrectly matched with number 1. According to the code table, letter M should be correctly matched with number 2. In the third pair, the letter D is incorrectly matched with number 2. According to the code table, letter D should be correctly matched with number 4. Since only one of the pairs is correctly matched, the answer is B.

23.   RSBMRM   759262
        GDSRVH   845730
        VDBRTM   349713

24.   TGVSDR   183247
        SMHRDP   520647
        TRMHSR   172057

25.   DSPRGM   456782
        MVDBHT   234902
        HPMDBT   062491

26. BVPTRD   936184   26._____
    GDPHMB   807029
    GMRHMV   827032

27. MGVRSH   283750   27._____
    TRDMBS   174295
    SPRMGV   567283

28. SGBSDM   489542   28._____
    MGHPTM   290612
    MPBMHT   269301

29. TDPBHM   146902   29._____
    VPBMRS   369275
    GDMBHM   842902

30. MVPTBV   236194   30._____
    PDRTMB   647128
    BGTMSM   981232

KEY (CORRECT ANSWERS)

1. A	11. B	21. C
2. C	12. C	22. B
3. B	13. D	23. B
4. D	14. D	24. B
5. D	15. D	25. C
6. B	16. C	26. A
7. B	17. D	27. D
8. B	18. A	28. A
9. A	19. B	29. D
10. C	20. A	30. A

TEST 2

DIRECTIONS: Each question or incomplete statement is followed by several suggested answers or completions. Select the one that BEST answers the question or completes the statement. *PRINT THE LETTER OF THE CORRECT ANSWER IN THE SPACE AT THE RIGHT.*

Questions 1-10

DIRECTIONS: Questions 1 through 10 each consist of two columns, each containing four lines of names, numbers and/or addresses. For each question, compare the lines in Column I with the lines in Column II to see if they match exactly, and mark your answer according to the following instructions:
- A. all four lines match exactly
- B. only three lines match exactly
- C. only two lines match exactly
- D. only one line matches exactly

	Column I	Column II	
1.	Earl Hodgson 1409870 Shore Ave. Macon Rd.	Earl Hodgson 1408970 Schore Ave. Macon Rd.	1.____
2.	9671485 470 Astor Court Halprin, Phillip Frank D. Poliseo	9671485 470 Astor Court Halperin, Phillip Frank D. Poliseo	2.____
3.	Tandem Associates 144-17 Northern Blvd. Alberta Forchi Kings Park, NY 10751	Tandom Associates 144-17 Northern Blvd. Albert Forchi Kings Point, NY 10751	3.____
4.	Bertha C. McCormack Clayton, MO 976-4242 New City, NY 10951	Bertha C. McCormack Clayton, MO 976-4242 New City, NY 10951	4.____
5.	George C. Morill Columbia, SC 29201 Louis Ingham 3406 Forest Ave.	George C. Morrill Columbia, SD 29201 Louis Ingham 3406 Forest Ave.	5.____

6.	506 S. Elliott Pl. Herbert Hall 4712 Rockaway Pkway 169 E. 7 St.	506 S. Elliott Pl. Hurbert Hall 4712 Rockaway Pkway 169 E. 7 St.	6._____
7.	345 Park Ave. Colman Oven Corp. Robert Conte 6179846	345 Park Pl. Coleman Oven Corp. Robert Conti 6179846	7._____
8.	Grigori Schierber Des Moines, Iowa Gouverneur Hospital 91-35 Cresskill Pl.	Grigori Schierber Des Moines, Iowa Gouverneur Hospital 91-35 Cresskill Pl.	8._____
9.	Jeffery Janssen 8041071 40 Rockefeller Plaza 407 6 St.	Jeffrey Janssen 8041071 40 Rockafeller Plaza 406 7 St.	9._____
10.	5971996 3113 Knickerbocker Ave. 8434 Boston Post Rd. Penn Station	5871996 3113 Knickerbocker Ave. 8424 Boston Post Rd. Penn Station	10._____

Questions 11-14

DIRECTIONS: Questions 11 through 14 are to be answered by looking at the four groups of names and addresses listed below and then finding out the number of groups that have their corresponding numbered lines exactly the same.

	GROUP I	GROUP II
Line 1:	Richmond General Hospital	Richman General Hospital
Line 2:	Geriatric Clinic	Geriatric Clinic
Line 3:	3975 Paerdegat St.	3975 Peardegat St.
Line 4:	Loudonville, New York 11538	Londonville, New York 11538

	GROUP III	GROUP IV
Line 1:	Richmond General Hospital	Richmend General Hospital
Line 2:	Geriatric Clinic	Geriatric Clinic
Line 3:	3795 Paerdegat St.	3975 Paerdegat St.
Line 4:	Loudonville, New York 11358	Loudonville, New York 11538

11. In how many groups is line 1 exactly the same?   11._____
    A. 2   B. 3   C. 4   D. None

12. In how many groups is line 2 exactly the same?   12._____
    A. 2   B. 3   C. 4   D. None

13. In how many groups is line 3 exactly the same?   13._____
    A. 2   B. 3   C. 4   D. None

14. In how many groups is line 4 exactly the same?   14._____
    A. 2   B. 3   C. 4   D. None

Questions 15-18

DIRECTIONS: Each of questions 15 through 18 has two lists of names and addresses. Each list contains three sets of names and addresses. Check each of the three sets in the list on the right to see if they are the same as the corresponding set in the list on the left. Mark your answers as follows:
A. if none of the sets are the same
B. if only one of the sets is the same
C. if only two of the sets are the same
D. if all three of the sets are the same

15. Mary T. Berlinger   Mary T. Berlinger   15._____
    2351 Hampton St.   2351 Hampton St.
    Monsey, NY 20117   Monsey, NY 20117

    Eduardo Benes   Eduardo Benes
    473 Kingston Avenue   473 Kingston Avenue
    Central Islip, NY 11734   Central Islip, NY 11734

    Alan Carrington Fuchs   Alan Carrington Fuchs
    17 Gnarled Hollow Road   17 Gnarled Hollow Road
    Los Angeles, CA 91635   Los Angeles, CA 91685

16. David John Jacobson   David John Jacobson   16._____
    178 35 St. Apt. 4C   178 53 St. Apt. 4C
    New York, NY 00927   New York, NY 00927

    Ann-Marie Calonella   Ann-Marie Calonella
    7243 South Ridge Blvd.   7243 South Ridge Blvd.
    Bakersfield, CA 96714   Bakersfield, CA 96714

    Pauline M. Thompson   Pauline M. Thomson
    872 Linden Ave.   872 Linden Ave.
    Houston, Texas 70321   Houston, Texas 70321

17. Chester LeRoy Masterton   Chester LeRoy Masterson   17._____
    152 Lacy Rd.   152 Lacy Rd.
    Kankakee, Ill. 54532   Kankakee, Ill. 54532

    William Maloney   William Maloney
    S. LaCrosse Pla.   S. LaCross Pla.
    Wausau, Wisconsin 52146   Wausau, Wisconsin 52146

    Cynthia V. Barnes   Cynthia V. Barnes
    16 Pines Rd.   16 Pines Rd.
    Greenpoint, Miss. 20376   Greenpoint, Miss. 20376

18. Marcel Jean Frontenac   Marcel Jean Frontenac   18._____
    8 Burton On The Water   6 Burton On The Water
    Calender, Me. 01471   Calender, Me. 01471

    J. Scott Marsden   J. Scott Marsden
    174 S. Tipton St.   174 Tipton St.
    Cleveland, Ohio   Cleveland, Ohio

    Lawrence T. Haney   Lawrence T. Haney
    171 McDonough St.   171 McDonough St.
    Decatur, GA 31304   Decatur, GA 31304

Questions 19-26

DIRECTIONS: Each of questions 19 through 26 has two lists of numbers. Each list contains three sets of numbers. Check each of the three sets in the list on the right to see if they are the same as the corresponding set in the list on the left. Mark your answers as follows:
- A. if none of the sets are the same
- B. if only one of the sets is the same
- C. if only two of the sets are the same
- D. if all three of the sets are the same

19. 7354183476   7354983476   19._____
    4474747744   4474747774
    57914302311   57914302311

20. 7143592185   7143892185   20._____
    8344517699   8344518699
    9178531263   9178531263

21. 2572114731   257214731   21._____
    8806835476   8806835476
    8255831246   8255831246

22.   331476853821   331476858621   22._____
        6976658532996   6976655832996
        3766042113715   3766042113745

23.   8806663315   8806663315   23._____
        74477138449   74477138449
        211756663666   211756663666

24.   990006966996   99000696996   24._____
        53022219743   53022219843
        4171171117717   4171171177717

25.   24400222433004   24400222433004   25._____
        5300030055000355   5300030055500355
        20000075532002022   20000075532002022

26.   61116664066001116   61116664066001116   26._____
        7111300117001100733   7111300117001100733
        26666446664476518   26666446664476518

Questions 27-30

DIRECTIONS: Questions 27 through 30 are to be answered by picking the answer which is in the correct numerical order, from the lowest to highest number, in each question.

27.   A. 44533, 44518, 44516, 44547   27._____
        B. 44516, 44518, 44533, 44547
        C. 44547, 44533, 44518, 44516
        D. 44518, 44516, 44547, 44533

28.   A. 95587, 95593, 95601, 95620   28._____
        B. 95601, 95620, 95587, 95593
        C. 95593, 95587, 95601, 95620
        D. 95620, 95601, 95593, 95587

29.   A. 232212, 232208, 232232, 232223   29._____
        B. 232208, 232223, 232212, 232232
        C. 232208, 232212, 232223, 232232
        D. 232223, 232232, 232208, 232212

30.   A. 113419, 113521, 113462, 113588   30._____
        B. 113588, 113462, 113521, 113419
        C. 113521, 113588, 113419, 113462
        D. 113419, 113462, 113521, 113588

KEY (CORRECT ANSWERS)

1. C	11. A	21. C
2. B	12. C	22. A
3. D	13. A	23. D
4. A	14. A	24. A
5. C	15. C	25. C
6. B	16. B	26. C
7. D	17. B	27. B
8. A	18. B	28. A
9. D	19. B	29. C
10. C	20. B	30. D

BASIC FUNDAMENTALS OF FILING SCIENCE

I. COMMENTARY

Filing is the systematic arrangement and storage of papers, cards, forms, catalogues, etc., so that they may be found easily and quickly. The importance of an efficient filing system cannot be emphasized too strongly. The filed materials form records which may be needed quickly to settle questions that may cause embarrassing situations if such evidence is not available. In addition to keeping papers in order so that they are readily available. the filing system must also be designed to keep papers in good condition. A filing system must be planned so that papers may be filed easily, withdrawn easily, and as quickly returned to their proper place. The cost of a filing system is also an important factor.

The need for a filing system arose when the business man began to carry on negotiations on a large scale. He could no longer be intimate with the details of his business. What was needed in the early era was a spindle or pigeon-hole desk. Filing in pigeon-hole desks is now almost completely extinct. It was an unsatisfactory practice since pigeon holes were not labeled, and the desk was an untidy mess.

II. BASIS OF FILING

The science of filing is an exact one and entails a thorough understanding of basic facts, materials, and methods. An overview of this important information now follows.

1. <u>Types of files</u>

   (1) SHANNON FILE
   This consists of a board, at one end of which are fastened two arches which may be opened laterally.

   (2) SPINDLE FILE
   This consists of a metal or wood base to which is attached a long, pointed spike. Papers are pushed down on the spike as received. This file is useful for temporary retention of papers.

   (3) BOX FILE
   This is a heavy cardboard or metal box, opening from the side like a book.

   (4) FLAT FILE
   This consists of a series of shallow drawers or trays, arranged like drawers in a cabinet.

   (5) BELLOWS FILE
   This is a heavy cardboard container with alphabetized or compartment sections, the ends of which are closed in such a manner that they resemble an accordion.

   (6) VERTICAL FILE
   This consists of one or more drawers in which the papers are stood on edge, usually in folders, and are indexed by guides. A series of two or more drawers in one unit is the usual file cabinet.

   (7) CLIP FILE
   This file has a large clip attached to a board and is very similar to the *SHANNON FILE*.

   (8) VISIBLE FILE
   Cards are filed flat in an overlapping arrangement which leaves a part of each card visible at all times.

(9) ROTARY FILE

The *ROTARY FILE* has a number of visible card files attached to a post around which they can be revolved. The wheel file has visible cards which rotate around a horizontal axle.

(10) TICKLER FILE

This consists of cards or folders marked with the days of the month, in which materials are filed and turned up on the appropriate day of the month.

2. <u>Aids in filing</u>

(1) GUIDES

Guides are heavy cardboard, pasteboard, or bristolboard sheets the same size as folders. At the top is a tab on which is marked or printed the distinguishing letter, words, or numbers indicating the material filed in a section of the drawe

(2) SORTING TRAYS

Sorting trays are equipped with alphabetical guides to facilitate the sorting of papers preparatory to placing them in a file.

(3) CODING

Once the classification or indexing caption has been determined, it must be indicated on the letter for filing purpose

(4) CROSS REFERENCE

Some letters or papers might easily be called for under two or more captions. For this purpose, a cross-reference card or sheet is placed in the folder or in the index.

3. <u>Variations of filing systems</u>

(1) VARIADEX ALPHABETIC INDEX

Provides for more effective expansion of the alphabetic system.

(2) TRIPLE-CHECK NUMERIC FILING

Entails a multiple cross-reference, as the name implies.

(3) VARIADEX FILING

Makes use of color as an aid in filing.

(4) DEWEY DECIMAL SYSTEM

The system is a numeric one used in libraries or for filing library materials in an office. This special type of filing system is used where material is grouped in finely divided categories, such as in libraries. With this method, all material to be filed is divided into ten major groups, from 000 to 900, and then subdivided into tens, units, and decimals.

4. <u>Centralized filing</u>

Centralized filing means keeping the files in one specific or central location. Decentralized filing means putting away papers in files of individual departments. The first step in the organization of a central filing department is to make a careful canvass of all desks in the offices. In this manner we can determine just what material needs to be filed, and what information each desk occupant requires from the central file. Only papers which may be used at some time by persons in the various offices should be placed in the central file. A paper that is to be used at some time by persons in the various offices should be placed in the central file. A paper that is to be used by one department only should never be filed in the central file.

5. <u>Methods of filing</u>

While there are various methods used for filing, actually there are only five basic systems: alphabetical, subject, numerical, geographic, and chronological. All other systems are derived from one of these or from a combination of two or more of them.

Since the purpose of a filing system is to store business records <u>systemically</u> so that any particular record can be found almost instantly when required, filing requires, in addition to the proper kinds of equipment and supplies, an effective method of indexing.

There are five basic systems of filing:

   (1) *ALPHABETIC FILING*

Most filing is alphabetical. Other methods, as described below, require extensive alphabetization.

In alphabetic filing, lettered dividers or guides are arranged in alphabetic sequence. Material to be filed is placed behind the proper guide. All materials under each letter are also arranged alphabetically. Folders are used unless the file is a card index.

   (2) *SUBJECT FILING*

This method is used when a single, complete file on a certain subject is desired. A subject file is often maintained to assemble all correspondence on a certain subject. Such files are valuable in connection with insurance claims, contract negotiations, personnel, and other investigations, special programs, and similar subjects.

   (3) *GEOGRAPHICAL FILE*

Materials are filed according to location: states, cities, counties, or other subdivisions. Statistics and tax information are often filed in this manner.

   (4) *CHRONOLOGICAL FILE*

Records are filed according to date. This method is used especially in "tickler" files that have guides numbered 1 to 31 for each day of the month. Each number indicates the day of the month when the filed item requires attention.

   (5) *NUMERICAL FILE*

This method requires an alphabetic card index giving name and number. The card index is used to locate records numbered consecutively in the files according to date received or sequence in which issued, such as licenses, permits, etc.

6. <u>Indexing</u>

Determining the name or title under which an item is to be filed is known as <u>indexing</u>. For example, how would a letter from Robert E. Smith be filed? The name would be rearranged Smith, Robert E., so that the letter would be filed under the last name.

7. <u>Alphabetizing</u>

The arranging of names for filing is known as <u>alphabetizing</u>. For example, suppose you have four letters indexed under the names Johnson, Becker, Roe, and Stern. How should these letters be arranged in the files so that they may be found easily? You would arrange the four names alphabetically, thus, Becker, Johnson, Roe, and Stern.

III. RULES FOR INDEXING AND ALPHABETIZING
1. The names of persons are to be transposed. Write the surname first, then the given name, and, finally, the middle name or initial. Then arrange the various names according to the alphabetic order of letters throughout the entire name. If there is a title, consider that after the middle name or initial.

NAMES	INDEXED AS
Arthur L. Bright	Bright, Arthur L.
Arthur S. Bright	Bright, Arthur S.
P.E. Cole	Cole, P.E.
Dr. John C. Fox	Fox, John C. (Dr.)

2. If a surname includes the same letters of another surname, with one or more additional letters added to the end, the shorter surname is placed first regardless of the given name or the initial of the given name.

NAMES	INDEXED AS
Robert E. Brown	Brown, Robert E.
Gerald A. Browne	Browne, Gerald A.
William O. Brownell	Brownell, William O.

3. Firm names are alphabetized under the surnames. Words like the, an, a, of, and for, are not considered.

NAMES	INDEXED AS
Bank of America	Bank of America
Bank Discount Dept.	Bank Discount Dept.
The Cranford Press	Cranford Press, The
Nelson Dwyer & Co.	Dwyer, Nelson, & Co.
Sears, Roebuck & Co.	Sears, Roebuck & Co.
Montgomery Ward & Co.	Ward, Montgomery, & Co.

4. The order of filing is determined first of all by the first letter of the names to be filed. If the first letters are the same, the order is determined by the second letters, and so on. In the following pairs of names, the order is determined by the letters underlined:

A_u_sten	H_a_yes	Ha_n_son	Har_v_ey	Heat_h_	Gree_n_	Schwar_tz_
B_a_ker	H_e_ath	Ha_r_per	Har_w_ood	Heat_on_	Gree_ne_	Schwar_z_

5. When surnames are alike, those with initials only precede those with given names, unless the first initial comes alphabetically after the first letter of the name.

   Gleason, S.   *but,* Abbott, Mary
   Gleason, S.W.   Abbott, W.B.
   Gleason, Sidney

6. Hyphenated names are treated as if spelled without the hyphen.

   Lloyd, Paul N.   Lloyd, Robert
   Lloyd-Jones, James   Lloyd-Thomas, A.S.

7. Company names composed of single letters which are not used as abbreviations precede the other names beginning with the same letter.

   B & S Garage   E Z Duplicator Co.
   B X Cable Co.   Eagle Typewriter Co.
   Babbitt, R.N.   Edison Company

8. The ampersand (&) and the apostrophe (') in firm names are disregarded in alphabetizing.

   Nelson & Niller   M & C Amusement Corp.
   Nelson, Walter J.   M C Art Assn.
   Nelson's Bakery

9. Names beginning with Mac, Mc, or M' are usually placed in regular order as spelled. Some filing systems file separately names beginning with Mc.

   MacDonald, R.J.   Mazza, Anthony
   Macdonald, S.B.   McAdam, Wm.
   Mace, Wm.   McAndrews, Jerry

10. Names beginning with St. are listed as if the name Saint were spelled in full. Numbered street names and all abbreviated names are treated as if spelled out in full.

    Saginaw   Fifth Avenue Hotel   Hart Mfg. Co.
    St. Louis   42nd Street Dress Shop   Hart, Martin
    St. Peter's Rectory Hart, Chas.   Hart, Thos.
    Sandford   Hart, Charlotte   Hart, Thomas A.
    Smith, Wm.   Hart, Jas.   Hart, Thos. R.
    Smith, Willis   Hart, Janice

11. Federal, state, or city departments of government should be placed alphabetically under the governmental branch controlling them.

    Illinois, State of -- Departments and Commissions
       Banking Dept.
       Employment Bureau
    United States Government Departments
       Commerce
       Defense
       State
       Treasury

12. Alphabetic order
    Each word in a name is an indexing unit. Arrange the names in alphabetic order by comparing similar units in each name. Consider the second units only when the first units are identical. Consider the third units only when both the first and second units are identical.

13. Single surnames or initials
    A surname, when used alone, precedes the same surname with a first name or initial. A surname with a first initial only precedes a surname with a complete first name. This rule is sometimes stated,"nothing comes before something."

14. Surname prefixes
    A surname prefix is not a separate indexing unit, but it is considered part of the surname. These prefixes include: d', D', Da, de, De, Del, Des, Di, Du, Fitz., La, Le, Mc, Mac, 'c, O', St., Van, Van der, Von, Von der, and others. The prefixes M', Mac, and Mc are indexed and filed exactly as they are spelled.

15. Names of firms
    Names of firms and institutions are indexed and filed exactly as they are written when they do not contain the complete name of an individual.

16. Names of firms containing complete individual names
    When the firm or institution name includes the complete name of an individual, the units are transposed for indexing in the same way as the name of an individual.

17. Article "The"
    When the article <u>the</u> occurs at the beginning of a name, it is placed at the end in parentheses but it is not moved. In both cases, it is not an indexing unit and is disregarded in filing.

18. Hyphenated names
    Hyphenated firm names are considered as separate indexing units. Hyphenated surnames of individuals are considered as one indexing unit; this applies also to hyphenated names of individuals whose complete names are part of a firm name.

19. Abbreviations

    Abbreviations are considered as though the name were written in full; however, single letters other than abbreviations are considered as separate indexing units.

20. Conjunctions, prepositions and firm endings

    Conjunctions and prepositions, such as and, for, in, of, are disregarded in indexing and filing but are not omitted or their order changed when writing names on cards and folders. Firm endings such as Ltd., Inc., Co., Son, Bros., Mfg., and Corp., are treated as a unit in indexing and filing and are considered as though spelled in full, such as Brothers and Incorporated.

21. One or two words

    Names that may be spelled either as one or two words are indexed and filed as one word.

22. Compound geographic names

    Compound geographic names are considered as separate indexing and filing units, except when the first part of the name is not an English word, such as the Los in Los Angeles.

23. Titles or degrees of individuals, whether preceding or following the name, are not considered in indexing or filing. They are placed in parentheses after the given name or initial. Terms that designate seniority, such as Jr., Sr., 2d, are also placed in parentheses and are considered for indexing and filing only when the names to be indexed are otherwise identical.

    <u>Exception A:</u>

    When the name of an individual consists of a title and one name only, such as Queen Elizabeth, it is not transposed and the title is considered for indexing and filing.

    <u>Exception B:</u>

    When a title or foreign article is the initial word of a firm or association name, it is considered for indexing and filing.

24. Possessives

    When a word ends in apostrophe s, the s is not considered in indexing and filing. However, when a word ends in s apostrophe, because the s is part of the original word, it is considered. This rule is sometimes stated, "Consider everything up to the apostrophe."

25. United States and foreign government names

    Names pertaining to the federal government are indexed and filed under United States Government and then subdivided by title of the department, bureau, division, commission, or board. Names pertaining to foreign governments are indexed and filed under names of countries and then subdivided by title of the department, bureau, division, commission, or board. Phrases, such as department of, bureau of, division of, commission of, board of, when used in titles of governmental bodies, are placed in parentheses after the word they modify, but are disregarded in indexing and filing. Such phrases, however, are considered in indexing and filing nongovernmental names.

26. Other political subdivisions

    Names pertaining to other political subdivisions, such as states, counties, cities, or towns, are indexed and filed under the name of the political subdivision and then subdivided by the title of the department, bureau, division, commission, or board.

27. Addresses

When the same name appears with different addresses, the names are indexed as usual and arranged alphabetically according to city or town. The State is considered only when there is duplication of both individual or company name and city name. If the same name is located at different addresses within the same city, then the names are arranged alphabetically by streets. If the same name is located at more than one address on the same street, then the names are arranged from the lower to the higher street number.

28. Numbers

Any number in a name is considered as though it were written in words, and it is indexed and filed as one unit.

29. Bank names

Because the names of many banking institutions are alike in several respects, as first National Bank, Second National Bank, etc., banks are indexed and filed first by city location, then by bank name, with the state location written in parentheses and considered only if necessary

30. Married women

The legal name of a married woman is the one used for filing purposes. Legally, a man's surname is the only part of a man's name a woman assumes when she marries. Her legal name, therefore, could be either:
   (1) Her own first and middle names together with her husband's surname, or
   (2) Her own first name and maiden surname, together with her husband's surname.

Mrs. is placed in parentheses at the end of the name. Her husband's first and middle names are given in parentheses below her legal name.

31. An alphabetically arranged list of names illustrating many difficult points of alphabetizing follows.

COLUMN I
Abbot, W.B.
Abbott, Alice
Allen, Alexander B.
Allen, Alexander B., Inc.
Andersen, Hans
Andersen, Hans E.
Andersen, Hans E., Jr.
Anderson, Andrew
Andrews, George
Brown Motor Co., Boston
Brown Motor Co., Chicago
Brown Motor Co., Philadelphia
Brown Motor Co., San Francisco
Dean, Anna
Dean, Anna F.
Dean, Anna Frances
Dean & Co.
Deane-Arnold Apartments
Deane's Pharmacy
Deans, Felix A.
Dean's Studio
Deans, Wm.
Deans & Williams
East Randolph
East St. Louis
Easton, Pa.
Eastport, Me.

COLUMN II
54th St. Tailor Shop
Forstall, W.J.
44th St. Garage
M A Delivery Co.
M & C Amusement Corp.
M C Art Assn.
MacAdam, Wm.
Macaulay, James
MacAulay, Wilson
MacDonald, R.J.
Macdonald, S.B.
Mace, Wm.
MacMahon, L.S.
Madison, Seth
Mazza, Anthony
McAdam, Wm.
McAndrews, Jerry
Meade & Clark Co.
Meade, S.T.
Meade, Solomon
Sackett Publishing Co.
Sacks, Robert
St. Andrew Hotel
St. John, Homer W.
Saks, Isaac B.
Stephens, Ira
Stevens, Delevan
Stevens, Delila

IV. OFFICIAL EXAMINATION DIRECTIONS AND RULES

To preclude the possibility of conflicting or varying methods of filing, explicit directions and express rules are given to the candidate before he answers the filing questions on an examination.

The most recent official directions and rules for the filing questions are given immediately hereafter.

OFFICIAL DIRECTIONS

Each of questions ... to ... consists of four(five)names. For each question, select the one of the four(five)names that should be first (second)(third)(last) if the four(five)names were arranged in alphabetical order in accordance with the rules for alphabetical filing given below. Read these rules carefully. Then, for each question, indicate in the correspondingly numbered row on the answer sheet the letter preceding the name that should be first(second)(third)(last) in alphabetical order.

OFFICIAL RULES FOR ALPHABETICAL FILING

Names of Individuals

1. The names of individuals are filed in strict alphabetical order first according to the last name, then according to first name or initial, and, finally, according to middle name or initial. For example: William Jones precedes George Kirk and Arthur S. Blake precedes Charles M. Blake.
2. When the last names are identical, the one with an initial instead of a first name precedes the one with a first name beginning with the same initial. For example: J.Green precedes Joseph Green.
3. When identical last names also have identical first names, the one without a middle name or initial precedes the one with a middle name or initial. For example: Robert Jackson precedes both Robert C.Jackson and Robert Chester Jackson.
4. When last names are identical and the first names are also identical, the one with a middle initial precedes the one with a middle name beginning with the same initial. For example: Peter A. Brown precedes Peter Alvin Brown.
5. Prefixes such as De, El, La, and Van are considered parts of the names they precede. For example: Wilfred DeWald precedes Alexander Duval.
6. Last names beginning with "Mac" or "Mc" are filed as spelled.
7. Abbreviated names are treated as if they were spelled out. For example: Jos. is filed as Joseph and Robt. is filed as Robert.
8. Titles and designations such as Dr., Mrs., Prof. are disregarded in filing.

Names of Business Organizations

1. The names of business organizations are filed exactly as written except that an organization bearing the name of an individual is filed alphabetically according to the name of the individual in accordance with the rules for filing names of individuals given above. For example: Thomas Allison Machine Company precedes Northern Baking Company.
2. When numerals occur in a name, they are treated as if they were spelled out. For example: 6 stands for six and 4th stands for fourth.
3. When the following words occur in names, they are disregarded: the, of, and. Sample: Choose the name that should be filed *third*.
   (A) Fred Town   (2)   (C) D. Town   (1)
   (B) Jack Towne   (3)   (D) Jack S.Towne (4)

The numbers in parentheses indicate the proper alphabetical order in which these names should be filed. Since the name that should be filed <u>third</u> is Jack Towne, the answer is (B).

FILING
Test 1

EXAMINATION SECTION
TEST 1

DIRECTIONS: Questions 1 through 8 each show in Column I names written on four cards (lettered w, x, y, z) which have to be filed. You are to choose the option (lettered A, B, C, or D) in Column II which BEST represents the proper order of filing according to the Rules for Alphabetic Filing, given before, and the sample question given below. Print the letter of the correct answer in the space at the right.

SAMPLE QUESTION

Column I	Column II
w. Jane Earl	A. w, y, z, x
x. James A. Earle	B. y, w, z, x
y. James Earl	C. x, y, w, z
z. J. Earle	D. x, w, y, z

The correct way to file the cards is:
- y. James Earl
- w. Jane Earl
- z. J. Earle
- x. James A. Earle

The correct filing order is shown by the letters, y, w, z, x (in that sequence). Since, in Column II, B appears in front of the letters, y, w, z, x (in that sequence), B is the correct answer to the sample question.

Now answer the following questions using that same procedure.

Column I	Column II	
1. w. James Rothschild x. Julius B. Rothchild y. B. Rothstein z. Brian Joel Rothenstein	A. x, z, w, y B. x, w, z, y C. z, y, w, x D. z, w, x, y	1. ...
2. w. George S. Wise x. S. G. Wise y. Geo. Stuart Wise z. Prof. Diana Wise	A. w, y, z, x B. x, w, y, z C. y, x, w, z D. z, w, y, x	2. ...
3. w. 10th Street Bus Terminal x. Buckingham Travel Agency y. The Buckingham Theater z. Burt Tompkins Studio	A. x, z, w, y B. y, x, w, z C. w, z, y, x D. x, w, y, z	3. ...
4. w. National Council of American Importers x. National Chain Co. of Providence y. National Council on Alcoholism z. National Chain Co.	A. w, y, x, z B. x, z, w, y C. z, x, w, y D. z, x, y, w	4. ...
5. w. Dr. Herbert Alvary x. Mr. Victor Alvarado y. Alvar Industries z. V. Alvarado	A. w, y, x, z B. z, w, x, y C. y, z, x, w D. w, z, x, y	5. ...
6. w. Joan MacBride x. Wm. Mackey y. Roslyn McKenzie z. Winifred Mackey	A. w, x, z, y B. w, y, z, x C. w, z, x, y D. w, y, x, z	6. ...

Column I	Column II	
7. w. 3 Way Trucking Co. x. 3rd Street Bakery y. 380 Realty Corp. z. Three Lions Pub	A. y, x, z, w B. y, z, w, x C. x, y, z, w D. x, y, w, z	7. ...
8. w. Miss Rose Leonard x. Rev. Leonard Lucas y. Sylvia Leonard Linen Shop z. Rose S. Leonard	A. z, w, x, y B. w, z, y, x C. w, x, z, y D. z, w, y, x	8. ...

TEST 2

DIRECTIONS: Questions 1 through 7 each show in Column I four names (lettered w, x, y, z) which have to be entered in an agency telephone directory. You are to choose the option (lettered A, B, C, or D) in Column II which *BEST* represents the proper order for entering them according to the Rules for Alphabetic Filing, given before, and the sample question given below.

SAMPLE QUESTION

Column I	Column II
w. Doris Jenkin x. Donald F. Jenkins y. Donald Jenkin z. D. Jenkins	A. w, y, z, x B. y, w, z, x C. x, y, w, z D. x, w, y, z

The correct way to enter these names is:
   y. Donald Jenkin
   w. Doris Jenkin
   z. D. Jenkins
   x. Donald F. Jenkins

The correct order is shown by the letters y, w, z, x, in that sequence. Since, in Column II, B appears in front of the letters y, w, z, x, in that sequence, B is the correct answer to the sample question.

Now answer the following questions using the same procedure.

Column I	Column II	
1. w. Lawrence Robertson x. Jack L. Robinson y. John Robinson z. William B. Roberson	A. x, y, w, z B. w, z, x, y C. z, w, x, y D. z, w, y, x	1. ...
2. w. P. N. Figueredo x. M. Alice Figueroa y. Jose Figueredo z. M. Alicia Figueroa	A. y, x, z, w B. x, z, w, y C. x, w, z, y D. y, w, x, z	2. ...
3. w. George Steven Keats x. George S. Keats y. G. Samuel Keats z. Dr. Samuel Keats	A. y, x, w, z B. z, y, x, w C. x, z, w, y D. w, z, x, y	3. ...
4. w. V. Merchant x. Dr. William Mercher y. Prof. Victor Merchant z. Dr. Walter Merchan	A. w, x, y, z B. w, y, z, x C. z, y, w, x D. z, w, y, x	4. ...

Column I	Column II	
5. w. Brian McCoy	A. z, x, y, w	5. ...
x. William Coyne	B. y, w, z, x	
y. Mr. William MacCoyle	C. x, z, y, w	
z. Dr. D. V. Coyne	D. w, y, z, x	
6. w. Ms. M. Rosie Buchanan	A. z, y, x, w	6. ...
x. Rosalyn M. Buchanan	B. w, z, x, y	
y. Rosie Maria Buchanan	C. w, z, y, x	
z. Rosa Marie Buchanan	D. z, x, y, w	
7. w. Prof. Jonathan Praga	A. w, z, y, x	7. ...
x. Dr. Joan Prager	B. w, x, z, y	
y. Alan VanPrague	C. x, w, z, y	
z. Alexander Prague	D. x, w, y, z	

TEST 3

DIRECTIONS: Questions 1 through 10 each show in Column I names written on four cards (lettered w, x, y, z) which have to be filed. You are to choose the option (lettered A, B, C, or D) in Column II which *BEST* represents the proper order of filing according to the rules and sample question given below. The cards are to be filed according to the Rules for Alphabetical Filing, given before, and the sample question given below.

SAMPLE QUESTION

Column I	Column II
w. Jane Earl	A. w, y, z, x
x. James A. Earle	B. y, w, z, x
y. James Earl	C. x, y, w, z
z. J. Earle	D. x, w, y, z

The correct way to file the cards is:
   y. James Earl
   w. Jane Earl
   z. J. Earle
   x. James A. Earle

The correct filing order is shown by the letters y, w, z, x (in that order). Since, in Column II, B appears in front of the letters y, w, z, x (in that order), B is the correct answer to the sample question.

Now answer Questions 1 through 10 using the same procedure.

Column I	Column II	
1. w. John Smith	A. w, x, y, z	1. ...
x. Joan Smythe	B. y, z, x, w	
y. Gerald Schmidt	C. y, z, w, x	
z. Gary Schmitt	D. z, y, w, x	
2. w. A. Black	A. w, x, y, z	2. ...
x. Alan S. Black	B. w, y, x, z	
y. Allan Black	C. w, y, z, x	
z. Allen A. Black	D. x, w, y, z	
3. w. Samuel Haynes	A. w, x, y, z	3. ...
x. Sam C. Haynes	B. x, w, z, y	
y. David Haynes	C. y, z, w, x	
z. Dave L. Haynes	D. z, y, x, w	

3

	Column I		Column II	
4.	w. Lisa B. McNeil	A.	x, y, w, z	4. ...
	x. Tom MacNeal	B.	x, z, y, w	
	y. Lisa McNeil	C.	y, w, z, x	
	z. Lorainne McNeal	D.	z, x, y, w	
5.	w. Larry Richardson	A.	w, y, x, z	5. ...
	x. Leroy Richards	B.	y, x, z, w	
	y. Larry S. Richards	C.	y, z, x, w	
	z. Leroy C. Richards	D.	x, w, z, y	
6.	w. Arlene Lane	A.	w, z, y, x	
	x. Arlene Cora Lane	B.	w, z, x, y	
	y. Arlene Clair Lane	C.	y, x, z, w	
	z. Arlene C. Lane	D.	z, y, w, x	
7.	w. Betty Fish	A.	w, x, z, y	7. ...
	x. Prof. Ann Fish	B.	x, w, y, z	
	y. Norma Fisch	C.	y, z, x, w	
	z. Dr. Richard Fisch	D.	z, y, w, x	
8.	w. Dr. Anthony David Lukak	A.	w, y, z, x	8. ...
	x. Mr. Steven Charles Lucas	B.	x, z, w, y	
	y. Mr. Anthony J. Lukak	C.	z, x, y, w	
	z. Prof. Steven C. Lucas	D.	z, x, w, y	
9.	w. Martha Y. Lind	A.	w, y, z, x	9. ...
	x. Mary Beth Linden	B.	w, y, x, z	
	y. Martha W. Lind	C.	y, w, z, x	
	z. Mary Bertha Linden	D.	y, w, x, z	
10.	w. Prof. Harry Michael MacPhelps	A.	w, z, x, y	10. ...
	x. Mr. Horace M. MacPherson	B.	w, y, z, x	
	y. Mr. Harold M. McPhelps	C.	z, x, w, y	
	z. Prof. Henry Martin MacPherson	D.	x, z, y, w	

TEST 4

DIRECTIONS: Answer Questions 1 through 5 on the basis of the following information:

A certain shop keeps an informational card file on all suppliers and merchandise. On each card is the supplier's name, the contract number for the merchandise he supplies, and a delivery date for the merchandise. In this filing system, the supplier's name is filed alphabetically, the contract number for the merchandise is filed numerically, and the delivery date is filed chronologically.

In Questions 1 through 5 there are five notations numbered 1 through 5 shown in Column I. Each notation is made up of a supplier's name, a contract number, and a date which is to be filed according to the following rules:

    First: File in alphabetical order;
    Second: When two or more notations have the same supplier, file according to the contract number in numerical order beginning with the lowest number;
    Third: When two or more notations have the same supplier and contract number, file according to the date beginning with the earliest date.

In Column II the numbers 1 through 5 are arranged in four ways to show four different orders in which the merchandise information might be filed. Pick the answer (A, B, C, or D) in Column II in which the notations are arranged according to the above filing rules.

SAMPLE QUESTION

Column I	Column II
1. Cluney (4865) 6/17/72	A. 2, 3, 4, 1, 5
2. Roster (2466) 5/10/71	B. 2, 5, 1, 3, 4
3. Altool (7114) 10/15/72	C. 3, 2, 1, 4, 5
4. Cluney (5296) 12/18/71	D. 3, 5, 1, 4, 2
5. Cluney (4865) 4/8/72	

The correct way to file the cards is:
 3. Altool (7114) 10/15/72
 5. Cluney (4865) 4/8/72
 1. Cluney (4865) 6/17/72
 4. Cluney (5276) 12/18/71
 2. Roster (2466) 5/10/71

Since the correct filing order is 3, 5, 1, 4, 2, the answer to the sample question is D. Now answer Questions 1 through 5.

	Column I		Column II	
1.	1. Warren (96063) 3/30/73	A. 2, 4, 3, 5, 1	1. ...
	2. Moore (21237) 9/4/74	B. 2, 3, 5, 4, 1	
	3. Newman (10050) 12/12/73	C. 4, 5, 2, 3, 1	
	4. Downs (81251) 1/2/73	D. 4, 2, 3, 5, 1	
	5. Oliver (60145) 6/30/74		
2.	1. Henry (40552) 7/6/74	A. 5, 4, 3, 1, 2	2. ...
	2. Boyd (91251) 9/1/73	B. 2, 3, 4, 1, 5	
	3. George (8196) 12/12/73	C. 2, 4, 3, 1, 5	
	4. George (31096) 1/12/74	D. 5, 2, 3, 1, 4	
	5. West (6109) 8/9/73		
3.	1. Salba (4670) 9/7/73	A. 5, 3, 1, 2, 4	3. ...
	2. Salba (51219) 3/1/73	B. 3, 1, 2, 4, 5	
	3. Crete (81562) 7/1/74	C. 3, 5, 4, 2, 1	
	4. Salba (51219) 1/11/74	D. 5, 3, 4, 2, 1	
	5. Texi (31549) 1/25/73		
4.	1. Crayone (87105) 6/10/74	A. 1, 2, 5, 3, 4	4. ...
	2. Shamba (49210) 1/5/73	B. 1, 5, 2, 3, 4	
	3. Valiant (3152) 5/1/74	C. 1, 5, 3, 4, 2	
	4. Valiant (3152) 1/9/74	D. 1, 5, 2, 4, 3	
	5. Poro (59613) 7/1/73		
5.	1. Mackie (42169) 12/20/73	A. 3, 2, 1, 5, 4	5. ...
	2. Lebo (5198) 9/12/72	B. 3, 2, 4, 5, 1	
	3. Drummon (99631) 9/9/74	C. 3, 5, 2, 4, 1	
	4. Lebo (15311) 1/25/72	D. 3, 5, 4, 2, 1	
	5. Harvin (81765) 6/2/73		

TEST 5

DIRECTIONS: Each of Questions 1 through 8 represents five cards to be filed, numbered 1 through 5 in Column I. Each card is made up of the employee's name, the date of a work assignment, and the work assignment code number shown in parentheses. The cards are to be filed according to the following rules:

First: File in alphabetical order;
Second: When two or more cards have the same employee's name, file according to the assignment date beginning with the earliest date;
Third: When two or more cards have the same employee's name and the same date, file according to the work assignment number beginning with the lowest number.

Column II shows the cards arranged in four different orders. Pick the answer (A, B, C, or D) in Column II which shows the cards arranged correctly according to the above filing rules.

SAMPLE QUESTION

	Column I			Column II
1.	Cluney	4/8/72	(486503)	A. 2, 3, 4, 1, 5
2.	Roster	5/10/71	(246611)	B. 2, 5, 1, 3, 4
3.	Altool	10/15/72	(711433)	C. 3, 2, 1, 4, 5
4.	Cluney	12/18/72	(527610)	D. 3, 5, 1, 4, 2
5.	Cluney	4/8/72	(486500)	

The correct way to file the cards is:

3.	Altool	10/15/72	(711433)
5.	Cluney	4/8/72	(486500)
1.	Cluney	4/8/72	(486503)
4.	Cluney	12/18/72	(527610)
2.	Roster	5/10/71	(246611)

The correct filing order is shown by the numbers in front of each name (3, 5, 1, 4, 2). The answer to the sample question is the letter in Column II in front of the numbers 3, 5, 1, 4, 2. This answer is D.

Now answer Questions 1 through 8 according to these rules.

		Column I			Column II	
1.	1.	Kohls	4/2/72	(125677)	A. 1, 2, 3, 4, 5	1. ...
	2.	Keller	3/21/72	(129698)	B. 3, 2, 1, 4, 5	
	3.	Jackson	4/10/72	(213541)	C. 3, 1, 2, 4, 5	
	4.	Richards	1/9/73	(347236)	D. 5, 2, 1, 3, 4	
	5.	Richmond	12/11/71	(379321)		
2.	1.	Burroughs	5/27/72	(237896)	A. 1, 4, 3, 2, 5	2. ...
	2.	Charlson	1/16/72	(114537)	B. 4, 1, 5, 3, 2	
	3.	Carlsen	12/2/72	(114377)	C. 1, 4, 3, 5, 2	
	4.	Burton	5/1/72	(227096)	D. 4, 1, 3, 5, 2	
	5.	Charlson	12/2/72	(114357)		
3.	1.	Ungerer	11/11/72	(537924)	A. 1, 5, 3, 2, 4	3. ...
	2.	Winters	11/10/72	(657834)	B. 5, 1, 3, 4, 2	
	3.	Ventura	12/1/72	(698694)	C. 3, 5, 1, 2, 4	
	4.	Winters	10/11/72	(675654)	D. 1, 5, 3, 4, 2	
	5.	Ungaro	11/10/72	(684325)		
4.	1.	Norton	3/12/73	(071605)	A. 1, 4, 2, 3, 5	4. ...
	2.	Morris	2/26/73	(068931)	B. 3, 5, 2, 4, 1	
	3.	Morse	5/12/73	(142358)	C. 2, 4, 3, 5, 1	
	4.	Morris	2/26/73	(068391)	D. 4, 2, 5, 3, 1	
	5.	Morse	2/26/73	(068391)		
5.	1.	Eger	4/19/72	(874129)	A. 3, 4, 1, 2, 5	5. ...
	2.	Eihler	5/19/73	(875329)	B. 1, 4, 5, 2, 3	
	3.	Ehrlich	11/19/72	(874839)	C. 4, 1, 3, 2, 5	
	4.	Eger	4/19/72	(876129)	D. 1, 4, 3, 5, 2	
	5.	Eihler	5/19/72	(874239)		

		Column I			Column II

6. 1. Johnson 12/21/72 (786814)   A. 2, 4, 3, 5, 1   6. ...
    2. Johns   12/21/73 (801024)   B. 4, 2, 5, 3, 1
    3. Johnson 12/12/73 (762814)   C. 4, 5, 3, 1, 2
    4. Jackson 12/12/73 (862934)   D. 5, 3, 1, 2, 4
    5. Johnson 12/12/73 (762184)
7. 1. Fuller   7/12/72   (598310)   A. 2, 1, 5, 4, 3   7. ...
    2. Fuller   7/2/72   (598301)   B. 1, 2, 4, 5, 3
    3. Fuller   7/22/72   (598410)   C. 1, 4, 5, 2, 3
    4. Fuller   7/17/73   (598710)   D. 2, 1, 3, 5, 4
    5. Fuller   7/17/73   (598701)
8. 1. Perrine 10/27/69 (637096)   A. 3, 4, 5, 1, 2   8. ...
    2. Perrone 11/14/72 (767609)   B. 3, 2, 5, 4, 1
    3. Perrault 10/15/68 (629706)   C. 5, 3, 4, 1, 2
    4. Perrine 10/17/72 (373656)   D. 4, 5, 1, 2, 3
    5. Perine   10/17/71 (376356)

TEST 6

DIRECTIONS FOR THIS SECTION:
Each question or incomplete statement is followed by several suggested answers or completions. Select the one that *BEST* answers the question or completes the statement. *PRINT THE LETTER OF THE CORRECT ANSWER IN THE SPACE AT THE RIGHT.*

1. *Which one* of the following BEST describes the usual arrangement of a tickler file?   1. ...
   A. Alphabetical   B. Chronological
   C. Numerical   D. Geographical

2. *Which one* of the following is the LEAST desirable filing practice?   2. ...
   A. Using staples to keep papers together
   B. Filing all material without regard to date
   C. Keeping a record of all materials removed from the files
   D. Writing filing instructions on each paper prior to filing

3. The *one* of the following records which it would be MOST advisable to keep in alphabetical order is a   3. ...
   A. continuous listing of phone messages, including time and caller, for your supervisor
   B. listing of individuals currently employed by your agency in a particular title
   C. record of purchases paid for by the petty cash fund
   D. dated record of employees who have borrowed material from the files in your office

4. Tickler systems are used in many legal offices for scheduling and calendar control. Of the following, the LEAST common use of a tickler system is to   4. ...
   A. keep papers filed in such a way that they may easily be retrieved
   B. arrange for the appearance of witnesses when they will be needed

C. remind lawyers when certain papers are due
D. arrange for the gathering of certain types of evidence

5. A type of file which permits the operator to remain   5. ...
seated while the file can be moved backward and forward
as required is BEST termed a
   A. lateral file   B. movable file
   C. reciprocating file   D. rotary file

6. In which of the following cases would it be MOST desirable   6. ...
to have two cards for one individual in a single alpha-
betic file? The individual has
   A. a hyphenated surname   B. two middle names
   C. a first name with an unusual spelling
   D. a compound first name

KEY (CORRECT ANSWERS)

TEST 1	TEST 2	TEST 3
1. A	1. C	1. C
2. D	2. D	2. A
3. B	3. A	3. D
4. D	4. D	4. B
5. C	5. A	5. B
6. A	6. B	6. A
7. C	7. B	7. C
8. B		8. D
		9. C
		10. A

TEST 4	TEST 5	TEST 6
1. D	1. B	1. B
2. B	2. A	2. B
3. B	3. B	3. B
4. D	4. D	4. A
5. C	5. D	5. C
	6. B	6. A
	7. D	
	8. C	

BASIC FUNDAMENTALS OF LIBRARY SCIENCE

CONTENTS

	PAGE
DEWEY DECIMAL SYSTEM	1
PREPARING TO USE THE LIBRARY	1
THREE TYPES OF BOOK CARDS	2
Author Card	2
Title Card	2
Subject Card	2
Call Number	2
PERIODICALS	3
PERIODICALS FILE	3
PERIODICAL INDEXES	3
TEST IN LIBRARY SCIENCE	4
I - Using a Card Catalog	4
II - Understanding Entries in a Periodical Index	5
III - Identifying Library Terms	6
IV - Finding a Book by Its Call Number	7
V - General	8
KEY (CORRECT ANSWERS)	8

BASIC FUNDAMENTALS OF LIBRARY SCIENCE

The problem of classifying all human knowledge has produced a branch of learning called "library science." A lasting contribution to a simple and understandable method of locating a book on any topic was designed by Melvil Dewey in 1876. His plan divided all knowledge into ten large classes and then dubdivided each class according to related groups.

DEWEY DECIMAL SYSTEM

1. Subject Classification

   The Dewey Decimal Classification System is the accepted and most widely used subject classification system in libraries throughout the world.

2. Classification by Three (3) Groups

   There are three groups of classification in the system. A basic group of ten (10) classifications arranges all knowledge as represented by books within groups by classifications numbered 000-900.

   The second group is the "100 division"; each group of the basic "10 divisions" is again divided into 9 sub-sctions allowing for more detailed and specialized subjects not identified in the 10 basic divisions.

3. There is a third, still further specialized "One thousand" group where each of the "100" classifications are further divided by decimalized, more specified, subject classifications. The "1,000" group is mainly used by highly specialized scientific and much diversified libraries.

These are the subject classes of the Dewey System:

- 000-099 General works (included bibliography, encyclopedias, collections, periodicals, newspapers, etc.)
- 100-199 Philosophy (includes psychology, logic, ethics, conduct, etc.)
- 200-299 Religion (includes mythology, natural theology, Bible, church history, etc.)
- 300-399 Social Science (includes economics, government, law, education, commerce, etc.)
- 400-499 Language (includes dictionaries, grammars, philology, etc.)
- 500-599 Science (includes mathematics, chemistry, physics, astronomy, geology, etc.)
- 600-699 Useful Arts (includes agriculture, engineering, aviation, medicine, manufactures, etc.)
- 700-799 Fine Arts (includes sculpture, painting, music, photography, gardening, etc.)
- 800-899 Literature (includes poetry, plays, orations, etc.)
- 900-999 History (includes geoegraphy, travel, biography, ancient and modern history, etc.)

PREPARING TO USE THE LIBRARY

Your ability to use the library and its resources is an important factor in determining your success. Skill and efficiency in finding the library materials you need for assignments and research papers will increase the amount of time you have to devote to reading or organizing information.

These are some of the preparations you can make now.

1. Develop skill in using your local library. You can increase your familiarity with the card catalog and the periodical indexes, such as the *Readers' Guide to Periodical Literature*, in any library.
2. Take the *Test in Library Science* to see how you can improve your knowledge of the library.

3. Read in such books as *Books, Libraries and You* by Jessie Edna Boyd, *The Library Key* by Margaret G. Cook, and *Making Books Work, a Guide to the Use of Libraries* by Jennie Maas Flexner.

You can find other titles by looking under the subject heading LIBRARIES AND READERS in the card catalog of your library.

THREE TYPES OF BOOK CARDS

Here are the three general types of cards which are used to represent a book in the main catalog.

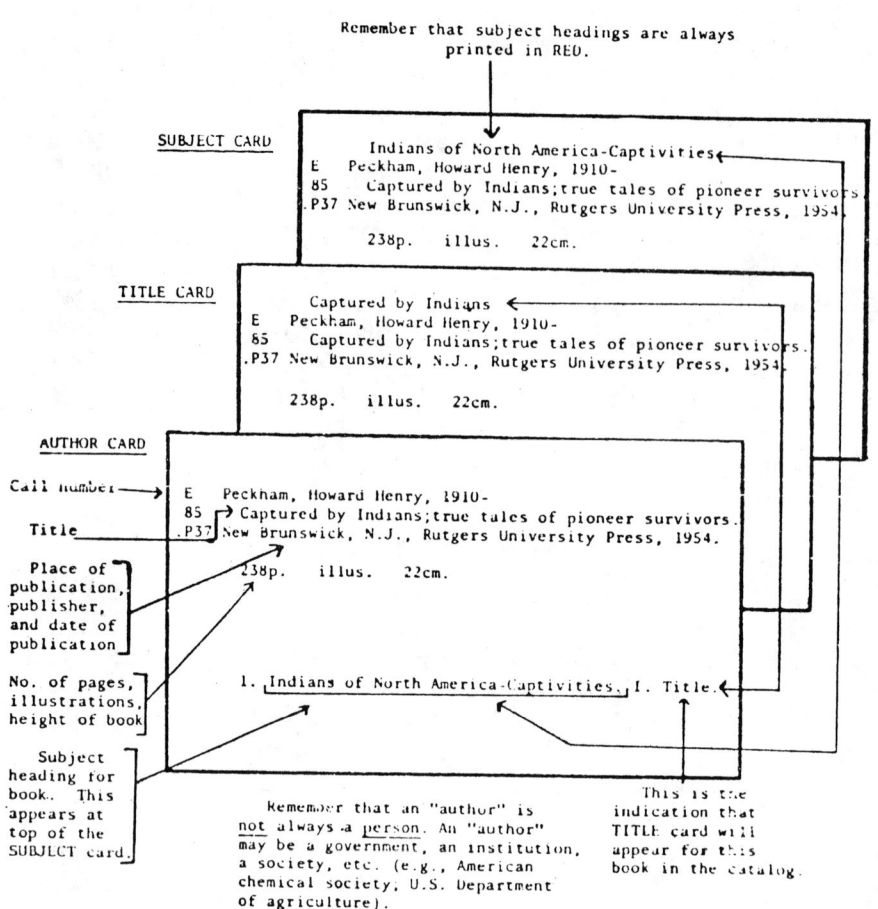

CARD CATALOG

The Card Catalog lists all books in the library by author. The majority of books also have title and subject cards.

<u>Author card</u>

If the author is known, look in the catalog under the author's name. The "author" for some works may be a society, an institution, or a government department.

<u>Title card</u>

Books with distinctive titles, anonymous works and periodicals will have a title card.

<u>Subject card</u>

To find books on a specific subject, look in the catalog under that subject heading. (Subject headings are printed in red on the Catalog Card.)

Call number
The letters and numbers in the upper left-hand corner of the Catalog Card are the book's call number. Copy this call number accurately, for it will determine the shelf location of the book. The word "Reference" marked in red in the upper right-hand corner of the catalog card indicates that the item is shelved in the Reference Section, and "Periodical" marked in yellow on the Catalog Card indicates that the item is shelved in the Periodicals Section.

PERIODICALS

All magazines are arranged in alphabetical order by title.

PERIODICALS FILE

To determine whether the Library has a specific magazine, consult the Periodicals File. Check the title of the magazine needed, and note that there are two cards for each title.

The bottom card lists the current issues available. The top card lists back bound volumes.

Those marked "Ask at Ref.Desk" may be obtained from the Reference Librarian.

PERIODICAL INDEXES

Material in magazines is more up-to-date than books and is a valuable source of information. To find articles on a chosen subject, use the periodical indexes.

The Readers' Guide to Periodical Literature is the most familiar of these indexes. In the front of each volume is a list of the periodicals indexed and a key to abbreviations. Similar aids appear in the front of other periodical indexes.

Sample entry: WEASELS
    WONDERFUL WHITE WEASEL. R.Beck. il OUTDOOR LIFE
    135:48-9+ Ja '65

Explanation : An illustrated article on the subject WEASELS entitled WONDERFUL WHITE WEASEL, by R.Beck, will be found in volume 135 of OUTDOOR LIFE, pages 48-9 (continued on later pages of the same issue),the January 1965 number.

Major libraries subscribe to the following indexes:

Art Index
Biography Index
Book Review Index
British Humanities Index
Essay and General Literature Index
  This is helpful for locating criticism of works of literature.
An Index to Book Reviews in the Humanities
International Index ceased publications June,1965 and continued
  as Social Science and Humanities Index
The Music Index
The New York Times Index
Nineteenth Century Readers' Guide
Poole's Index
Poverty and Human Resources Abstracts
Psychological Abstracts
Public Affairs Information Service, Bulletin of the (PAIS) is a subject index to current books, pamphlets, periodical articles, government documents, and other library materials in economics and public affairs.
Readers' Guide to Periodical Literature
Social Science and Humanities Index a continuation of the International Index
Sociological Abstracts

TEST IN LIBRARY SCIENCE

Do you have the basic skills for using a library efficiently? You should be able to answer AT LEAST 33 of the following questions correctly. *CHECK YOUR ANSWERS BY TURNING TO THE ANSWER KEY AT THE BACK OF THIS SECTION.*

I. USING A CARD CATALOG

Questions 1-9.

DIRECTIONS: An author card (or "main entry" card) is shown below. Identify each item on the card by selecting the CORRECT letters for them. *PRINT THE LETTER OF THE CORRECT ANSWER IN THE SPACE AT THE RIGHT.*

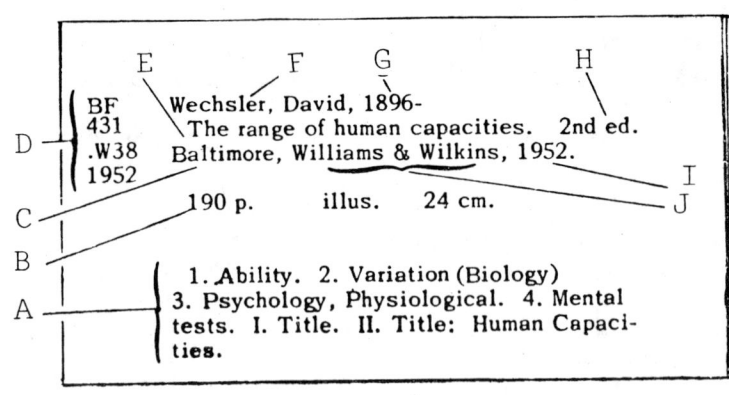

Sample Answer:
0. F

1. Date book was published.   1. ...
2. Number of pages in book.   2. ...
3. Title.   3. ...
4. Place of publication.   4. ...
5. Call number.   5. ...
6. Year author was born.   6. ...
7. Edition.   7. ...
8. Publisher.   8. ...
9. Other headings under which cards for this book may be   9. ...
   found.

Questions 10-13.

DIRECTIONS: Select the letter preceding the word or phrase which completes each of the following statements correctly.

10. The library's title card for the book THE LATE GEORGE AP-   10. ...
    LEY can be found by looking in the card catalog under
     A. Apley,George   B. The   C. Late   D. George   E. Apley
11. A catalog card for a book by John F. Kennedy would be   11. ...
    found in the drawer labelled
       A. JEFFERSON-JOHNSON,ROY
       B. PRESCOTT-PRICELESS
       C. KIERNAN-KLAY
       D. U.S.PRESIDENT-U.S.SOCIAL SECURITY
       E. KENNEBEC-KIERKEGAARD

4

12. The title cards for these three periodicals would be found   12. ...
    in the card catalog arranged in which of the following orders:
    A. NEW YORKER, NEWSWEEK, NEW YORK TIMES MAGAZINE
    B. NEWSWEEK, NEW YORKER, NEW YORK TIMES MAGAZINE
    C. NEW YORK TIMES MAGAZINE, NEW YORKER, NEWSWEEK
    D. NEW YORKER, NEW YORK TIMES MAGAZINE, NEWSWEEK
    E. NEWSWEEK, NEW YORK TIMES MAGAZINE, NEW YORKER
13. A card for a copy of the U.N.Charter would be found in the   13. ...
    catalog drawer marked
    A. TWENTIETH-UNAMUNO
    B. UNITED MINE WORKERS-UNITED SHOE MACHINERY
    C. U.S.BUREAU-U.S. CONGRESS
    D. U.S.SOCIAL POLICY-UNIVERSITAS
    E. CHANCEL-CIARDI

II. UNDERSTANDING ENTRIES IN A PERIODICAL INDEX
    Questions 14-25.
    DIRECTIONS: The following items are excerpts from THE READERS'
               GUIDE TO PERIODICAL LITERATURE. Identify each lettered
               section of the entries by placing the correct letters
               in the spaces. (There are more letters than spaces, so
               some of the letters will not be used.)

```
                              V
    A____UNITED NATIONS       |                    H_____Security Council
        Ambassador Goldberg holds news conference at    Security Council urged to respond to
        New York; transcript of conference,             challenge in southeast Asia; letter,
    B____July 28, 1965; with questions and answers.  U  M____July 30, 1965. A. J. Goldberg. Dept
        A. J. Goldberg. Dept. State Bul 53:272+              State Bul 53:278-80+  Ag 16, '65
    C____ Ag 16 '65                              T       |     |    |   |
        U.N. out of its teens. I.D. Talmadge. il Sr Schol-S      L   •I   J   K
    E____ 87:16-17+  S 16 '65
    D____ Whatever became of the United Nations?    Q
        America 113:235  S 4 '65
        F    R
                 Charter                          P
        Up-dating the pre-atomic United Nations; address,
        June 20, 1965. C.P. Romulo. Vital Speeches
        31:658-61 Ag 15 '65; Excerpts. Sat R 48:34-5+   O
        Jl 24 '65             N
                              G
```

14. Title of magazine containing a transcript of a news con-   14. ...
    conference held by U.N.Ambassador Arthur Goldberg.
15. Magazine in which the full text of C.P.Romulo's address   15. ...
    on the U.N. appears.
16. Author of an article titled U.N. OUT OF ITS TEENS.   16. ...
17. Date on which Ambassador Goldberg wrote a letter urging   17. ...
    the Security Council to respond to the challenge of south-
    east Asia.
18. Title of an article for which no author is listed.   18. ...
19. Date of the SATURDAY REVIEW issue which contains excerpts   19. ...
    of a speech called "Up-Dating the Pre-Atomic United Nations."
20. Pages in the DEPARTMENT OF STATE BULLETIN on which Am-   20. ...
    bassador Goldberg's letter appears.
21. Symbol indicating that the letter is continued on a la-   21. ...
    ter page.
22. Volume number of the magazine in which the article by   22. ...
    I.D.Talmadge is printed.
23. Symbols meaning September 16, 1965.   23. ...

24. The general subject heading under which all five articles   24. ...
    are listed.
25. A subject heading subdivision.   25. ...

Questions 26-27.

DIRECTIONS: Select the letter preceding the phrase which completes each of the following statements correctly.

26. To determine whether or not the library has THE MAGAZINE OF   26. ...
    AMERICAN HISTORY, check in
    A. the list of magazine titles in the front of THE READERS' GUIDE TO PERIODICAL LITERATURE
    B. the library's card catalog
    C. Ulrich's GUIDE TO PERIODICALS
    D. SATURDAY REVIEW
    E. THE LIBRARY JOURNAL

27. THE READERS' GUIDE is a good place to look for material on   27. ...
    the Job Corps because it
    A. indexes only the best books and magazines in each field
    B. is a guide to articles on many subjects appearing in all of the library's periodicals
    C. indexes recent discussions on the subject in many magazines
    D. specializes in official government information
    E. does all of the above

III. IDENTIFYING LIBRARY TERMS

Questions 28-32.

DIRECTIONS: Match the correct definitions with these terms by placing the correct letters in the blanks. (Some of the letters will not be used.)

28. Bibliography
29. Anthology
30. Index
31. Abstract
32. Subject heading

A. Word or phrase printed in red at the top of a catalog to indicate the major topic of the book
B. Brief written summary of the major ideas presented in an article or book
C. List of books and/or articles on one subject or by one author
D. Collection of selections from the writings of one or several authors
E. Written account of a person's life
F. Alphabetical list of subjects with the pages on which they are to be found in a book or periodical
G. Subordinate, usually explanatory title, additional to the main title and usually printed below it

28. ...
29. ...
30. ...
31. ...
32. ...

IV. FINDING A BOOK BY ITS CALL NUMBER

Questions 33-38.

DIRECTIONS: The Library of Congress classification system call numbers shown below are arranged in order, just as the books bearing those call numbers would be arranged on the shelves. To show where other call numbers would be located, select the letter of the CORRECT ANSWER.

A.	B.	C.	D.	E.	F.	G.	H.	I.	J.	K.
PS 201 .L67 1961	PS 201 .M44	PS 208 .B87 1944	PS 351 .D7	PS 351 .D77	PS 3513 .A2	PS 3515 .D72	PS 3515.3 A66	PS 3526 .N21	PS 3526.17 P2	PS 3526.37 A10

L.	M.	N.
PS 3526.37 C20	PS 3526.37 C37	PT 1 .R2

33. A book with the call number PS 201 .L67 would be shelved 33. ...
    A. Before A B. Between A & B C. Between B & C
    D. Between C & D E. Between D & E

34. A book with the call number PS 208 .B87 1944a would be shelved 34. ...
    A. Between A & B B. Between C & D C. Between B & C
    D. Between C & D E. Between D & E

35. A book with the call number PS 351 .D8 would be shelved 35. ...
    A. Between C & D B. Between D & E C. Between E & F
    D. Between F & G E. Between G & H

36. A book with the call number PS 3526.3 M53 would be shelved 36. ...
    A. Between L & M B. Between J & K C. Between K & L
    D. Between M & O E. Between O & P

37. A book with the call number PS 3526.37 C205 would be shelved 37. ...
    A. Between L & M B. Between N & O C. Between M & N
    D. Between O & P E. Between P & Q

38. A book with the call number PS 3526.37 C3 would be shelved 38. ...
    A. Between M & N B. Between L & M C. Between N & O
    D. Between O & P D. Between P & Q

V. General
   Questions 39-40.
   DIRECTIONS: Each question or incomplete statement is followed by several suggested answers or completions. Select the one that BEST answers the question or completes the statement. *PRINT THE LETTER OF THE CORRECT ANSWER IN THE SPACE AT THE RIGHT.*

39. When it is finished (in 610 volumes), the _____ will be the MOST monumental national bibliography in the world. 39. ..
    A. UNION LIST OF SERIALS IN LIBRARIES OF THE UNITED STATES AND CANADA
    B. UNITED STATES CATALOG
    C. READERS' GUIDE TO PERIODICAL LITERATURE
    D. NATIONAL UNION CATALOG

40. For those who wish to investigate the publishing companies and the people who control them, to locate the date a company was founded, who owned it, when it changed hands, what firm succeeded it, and other information of a similar nature, the periodical _____ is clearly invaluable. 40. ..
    A. PUBLISHERS' TRADE LIST ANNUAL (PTLA)
    B. CUMULATIVE BOOK INDEX
    C. AMERICAN BOOKTRADE DIRECTORY
    D. PUBLISHERS WEEKLY

KEY (CORRECT ANSWERS)

1. I   2. B   3. E   4. C   5. D   6. G   7. H   8. J   9. A
10. C - The first word of the title which is not an article.
11. E - Every book in the library is listed in the card catalog under the author's name. (Warning: The "author" may be a society, a university, or some other institution.)
12. C - A title is alphabetized word-by-word; therefore, "New" comes before "Newsweek," "New York" before "New Yorker."
13. B - The United Nations, not an individual, is the author of this work
14. T   16. Q   18. D   20. J   22. E   24. A   26. B   28. C   30. F   32. A
15. O   17. M   19. N   21. K   23. R   25. P/H   27. C   29. D   31. B
33. A - When two call numbers are identical except that one has a year or some other figure added at its end, the shorter call numbers comes first.
34. B
35. C - The numbers which follow a. are regarded as decimals; therefore .D77 precedes .D8.
36. B - 3526.3 precedes 3526.37
37. A - .C20 precedes .C205
38. B - .C3 precedes .C37
    (Read the call number line-by-line, and put a J before a P, before PB, etc. Put a lower number before a greater one.)
39. D
40. D

LIBRARY SCIENCE

TABLE OF CONTENTS

Chapter	Page
LIBRARIES AND LIBRARIANSHIP	1
BACKGROUND	1
Introduction	1
History of Libraries	1
Growth of Libraries in the United States	1
Professionalization	2
FACETS AND SCOPE OF LIBRARIANSHIP	2
Demand for Librarians in the Economy	2
Public Libraries	2
School Libraries	2
College and University Libraries	3
Special Libraries	3
The Modern Library	3
OCCUPATIONAL DESCRIPTIONS	4
Acquisitions Librarian	4
Bookmobile Driver	4
Bookmobile Librarian	5
Cataloger	5
Chief Librarian	6
Children's Librarian	6
Classifier	7
Collector, Overdue Material	7
Field Librarian	7
Film Librarian	8
Librarian	9
Librarian, Special Collections	9
Librarian, Special Library	10
Library Assistant	10
Library Associate Director	11
Library Director	11
Page	12
Patients' Librarian	12
Registration Clerk	12
School Librarian	13
Shelving Supervisor	13
Young Adult Librarian	13

LIBRARY SCIENCE

LIBRARIES AND LIBRARIANSHIP

A. BACKGROUND

INTRODUCTION

In the history of man, the communication of ideas has been the factor which distinguishes him from the lower animals. The ability to pass on knowledge and culture through the medium of speech led to the growth of civilization. Just as important, however, was the development of a means of preserving knowledge through written records, for it is this accumulated wealth of information which has enabled man to control his environment and to uncover some of the mysteries of the earth and heavens.

Throughout recorded history, it has been the duty of the librarian to preserve and organize the books and other records which contain man's knowledge and ideas so that they may be used most effectively to further the growth of civilization.

HISTORY OF LIBRARIES

Libraries have existed ever since man has written. Ancient Egypt boasted collections of papyrus rolls, while the Babylonians and Assyrians gathered together their cuneiform covered clay tablets so that they could be cataloged and preserved. Undoubtedly, the two most famous libraries of the ancient world were at Alexandria. In the third century B.C., only a few years after their founding, the larger of the two was reported to contain over a half million papyrus rolls. Some of the earliest experiments in bibliography were the catalogs of the Alexandrian libraries.

It was in ancient Rome that public libraries flourished in abundance and that the science of librarianship became recognized. The first large book collections were acquired as the spoils of war. The Romans realized their importance and enlarged them, in addition to building library collections of their own. In the fourth century, Rome had twenty-eight public libraries. With the fall of the Empire, however, books were withdrawn to monasteries and private collections. Not until the advent of the printing press in the middle of the fifteenth century did books again become plentiful and libraries again grow.

GROWTH OF LIBRARIES IN THE UNITED STATES

There have been books and libraries in the United States since the early days of the Colonies. The first organized library was founded in 1638 at Harvard University. As other colleges were instituted in the Colonies, they too established libraries for the use of their faculties and students. Public libraries did not come as quickly. The nearest approach to public library service was the subscription library, the first being Benjamin Franklin's Library Company, organized in Philadelphia in 1731. The first public library in the United States to be directly established by state legislation was the Boston library. In 1838, Massachusetts passed legislation specifically designed to allow the city of Boston to establish a public library and to appropriate municipal funds for its support. Earlier, Peterborough, New Hampshire, formed the first tax-supported library in 1833 on the basis of a state law passed in 1821 permitting a certain portion of tax revenue to be used for schools and other educational purposes.

PROFESSIONALIZATION

The years between 1850 and 1870 saw a period of rapid growth. Not only were college and public libraries flourishing, but governmental and specialized libraries achieved importance; and as the prestige of libraries grew, so did the role of the librarian and his responsibility. Librarianship became a profession in its own right. Realizing that librarians needed an organization to help them to utilize more fully the available materials and to standardize procedures, Melvil Dewey and other prominent members of the profession called a nationwide meeting of librarians in 1876, and the American Library Association was founded. This was the first of many professional organizations which have arisen to meet the needs of librarians in the ever-widening fields of knowledge which they serve.

B. FACETS AND SCOPE OF LIBRARIANSHIP

DEMAND FOR LIBRARIANS IN THE ECONOMY

As the scope of man's knowledge has increased and as the numbers of his written works have grown, so have libraries and the need for librarians. At the first meeting of the American Library Association in 1876, only one hundred and four persons were present. At that time, there were approximately 1,000 librarians in the United States. But, by 2001, it was estimated that there were more than 150,000 active professional librarians. Public libraries, colleges, and universities, schools, governmental agencies, public and private institutions, and commercial and industrial firms all have need of the librarian's services.

In general, it may be said that librarianship is a service profession, one in which the individual, no matter what his level of responsibility or specialization, devotes his time to satisfying the needs of others to obtain informational material. Because so many of the agencies, firms, and institutions cited above have realized the importance of having trained librarians administer to the needs of their staffs, faculties, students, or patrons, the demand for librarians continues to increase. According to the United States Department of Labor, the number of librarians is expected to increase by 4.9%, while library technicians increase by 13.4% and library assistants by 12.5% by 2014.

While the largest number of 2000 graduates (32%) were placed in college and university libraries, the need for librarians in many phases of activity can be seen from the fact that 29% of the graduates accepted positions in public libraries, 21% became school librarians, and 18% undertook special and other library work.

PUBLIC LIBRARIES

The public library in the United States today is a tax-supported institution, providing direct service to all members of the community. Informational, educational, and recreational materials are available, with special programs for work with children and young people, older persons, and adult education groups. The librarians involved in these programs must be knowledgeable as to the books and other materials available and the particular psychology of the age and social groups of the people whom they are serving.

SCHOOL LIBRARIES

The school library is established by the educational governing body, usually the Board of Education, in a school community to provide books and other educational materials to the children and faculties in the elementary and secondary schools. The librarian in a school library is usually required to have a background in educational theories as well as a degree in Library Science since he or she must provide supplementary teaching aids.

COLLEGE AND UNIVERSITY LIBRARIES

The college or university library, like the school library, is established to serve the particular community of an educational institution. Research materials are stressed. In the large universities, there may be several libraries, each one serving an individual college or department, i.e., the science library, medical school library, or art school library.

SPECIAL LIBRARIES

The field of special librarianship is widely diversified. In general, there are two types of special libraries: (1) The special organization library, serving all informational needs of an organization such as a corporation or governmental agency, in which both the staff and clientele are employees of the same organization; (2) the special subject library, which may be semi-public, independent, departmental, or branch library, serving students, professional groups, or members on a given subject. The special librarian must often be a specialist in a particular field of information. He must be aware of current publications and research, and be able to assemble, organize, and maintain this information so that it may be of greatest use to the library's clientele.

THE MODERN LIBRARY

The modern library, recognizing the many media of communication available today, includes a variety of materials in its collection. Not only are books and periodicals found on library shelves, but many institutions provide audio/video material, advanced media and Internet access to patrons, along with the records, films, and slides that remain vital even in today's advanced technological age. A few public libraries have framed paintings and other pictures which may be borrowed. Braille and talking books for the blind are available, as are ceiling-projected books for the bedridden.

Modern methods are used to increase library efficiency. Microfilm and digital copies of magazines and newspapers are important space-savers, as well as effective means of preserving information. Various systems of photographic charging of materials have resulted in a saving of man-hours and an elimination of many errors.

One of the newest ways in which libraries are utilizing modern science is in the use of automatic data processing systems for library cataloging and documentation. The introduction of these new systems has been brought about by the fact that in the second half of the 20th century and into the new millennium, the production of information has accelerated with startling speed and intensity. Approximately 50% of all scholarly material available today has been produced in the last fifteen years; there are now approximately 50,000 technical journals being published, and the number is expected to increase at the rate of 1,000 yearly; in scientific areas, it has been estimated that up to 2 million articles are published yearly.

New theories are being developed and new techniques are being applied to handle this flow of information. Complex electronic and mechanical means of information storage and retrieval are being developed to organize, catalog, classify, and index the wide diversity of information.

It is in the special library, the research library, and in specialized areas of the public library where the greatest concentration of information control has taken place. A number of organizations have created large information exchange networks, spanning the continent. In the future, it is expected that countries around the world will participate in the operation of information exchange systems.

OCCUPATIONAL DESCRIPTIONS

ACQUISITIONS LIBRARIAN
0-23.10
(100.288)

OCCUPATIONAL DEFINITION
Selects and orders books, periodicals, films, and other materials for library. Reviews publishers' announcements and catalogs, and compiles lists of publications to be purchased. Compares selections with card catalog and orders-in-process to avoid duplication. Circulates selection list to branches and departments for comments. Selects vendors on basis of such factors as discount allowances and delivery dates. Compiles statistics on purchases, such as total purchases, average price, and fund allocations. May recommend acquisition of materials from individuals or organizations or by exchange with other libraries. Collaborates daily with other units, with additional library staff, and with vendors and publishers to provide optimal access to library materials for the community. Will participate in providing materials budget estimates, establishing fund allocations, monitoring expenditures, and fiscal closing.

EDUCATIONAL AND TRAINING REQUIREMENTS
Master's degree in Library Science. Training time from 1 to 2 years.

BOOKMOBILE DRIVER
7-36.260
(109.368)

OCCUPATIONAL DEFINITION
Drives bookmobile or light truck that pulls book trailer, and assists in providing library services in mobile library. Drives vehicle to specified locations on predetermined schedule. Places books and periodicals on shelves according to such groupings as subject matter, readers' age grouping, or reading level. Stamps dates on library cards, files cards, and collects fines. Compiles reports of mileage, number of books issued, and amount of fines collected. Drives vehicle to garage for repairs, such as motor or transmission overhauls, and for preventive maintenance, such as chassis lubrication and oil change. Charges and discharges library material, in a timely manner. Assists patrons in locating appropriate library materials. Responds to ready reference questions. Takes application and issues library cards.

EDUCATIONAL AND TRAINING REQUIREMENTS
Tenth grade or above. Training time approximately two months.

BOOKMOBILE LIBRARIAN
0-23.20
(100.168)

OCCUPATIONAL DEFINITION
Provides library services for mobile library within given geographical area: Surveys community needs, and selects books and other materials for library. Publicizes visits to area to stimulate reading interest. May prepare special collections for schools and other groups. May arrange bookmobile schedule. May drive bookmobile. (This job is a specialization of LIBRARIAN and shares the same basic duties.)

EDUCATIONAL AND TRAINING REQUIREMENTS
Master's degree in Library Science. Training time – three months.

CATALOGER
0-23.10
(100.388)
catalog librarian; descriptive cataloger

OCCUPATIONAL DEFINITION
Compiles information on library materials, such as books and periodicals, and prepares catalog cards to identify materials and to integrate information into library catalog: Verifies author, title, and classification number on sample catalog card received from CLASSIFIER against corresponding data on title page. Fills in additional information, such as publisher, date of publication, and edition. Examines material and notes additional information, such as bibliographies, illustrations, maps, and appendices. Copies classification number from sample card into library material for identification. Files card in assigned sections of catalog. Tabulates number of sample cards according to quantity of material and catalog subject headings to determine number of new cards to be ordered or reproduced. Prepares inventory cards to record purchase information and location of library material. Requisitions additional cards. Records new information, such as death date of author and revised edition date, to amend cataloged cards. May specialize in regularly issued publications such as journals, periodicals, and bulletins, and be known as Serials Cataloger. In some instances, depending on the needs of the particular library system, the duties of CATALOGER and CLASSIFIER are combined into one occupation given the title of CATALOGER.

EDUCATIONAL AND TRAINING REQUIREMENTS
Master's degree in Library Science. Training time – one year.

CHIEF LIBRARIAN – BRANCH OR DEPARTMENT
0-23.20
(100.168)

OCCUPATIONAL DEFINITION
     Supervises staff, coordinates activities of library branch or department, and assists patrons in selection and location of books, films, audio/video items, web applications, and other materials: Trains and assigns duties to workers. Directs workers in performance of such tasks as receiving, shelving, and locating materials. Examines book reviews, publishers' catalogs, and other information sources to recommend material acquisition. Supervises and directs the arrangement of materials on shelves or in files according to classification codes, titles, or authors' names. Selects materials such as newspaper clippings and pictures to maintain special collections. Searches catalog files, biographical dictionaries, and indexes, and examines content of reference materials to assist patrons in locating and selecting materials. May assemble and arrange materials for display. May prepare replies to mail requests for information. May compile lists of library materials and recommend materials to individuals or groups and be designated Readers'-Advisory-Service Librarian. May be designated according to type of library as Chief Librarian, Branch; Chief Librarian, Bookmobile; or according to department as Chief Librarian, Art Department; Chief Librarian, Circulation Department; Chief Librarian, Music Department; Chief Librarian, Readers' Advisory Service.

EDUCATIONAL AND TRAINING REQUIREMENTS
Master's degree in Library Science. Training time of 2 to 4 years serving in various professional positions in a library system. Experience should reflect proven ability to supervise others.

CHILDREN'S LIBRARIAN
0-23.20
(100.168)

OCCUPATIONAL DEFINITION
     Assists children in selecting and locating library materials, and organizes and conducts activities for children to encourage reading and use of library facilities: Confers with teachers, parents, and community groups to relate library services to the concerns of adults working with children. Stimulates children's discriminate reading by organizing such activities as story hours, reading clubs, book fairs, and summer reading programs. Shows films, tells stories, and gives book talks to encourage reading. Conducts library tours to acquaint children with library facilities and services. (This job is a specialization of LIBRARIAN and shares the same basic duties.)

EDUCATIONAL AND TRAINING REQUIREMENTS
Master's degree in Library Science. Training time, six months to one year.

CLASSIFIER
0-23.10
(100.388)
subject cataloger

OCCUPATIONAL DEFINITION
	Classifies library materials such as books, films, audio/video material and periodicals according to subject matter: Reviews materials to be classified and searches information sources, such as book reviews, encyclopedias, online reference material and technical publications, to determine subject matter of materials.
	Selects classification numbers and descriptive headings according to Dewey Decimal, Library of Congress, or other library classification systems. Makes sample cards containing author, title, and classification number to guide CATALOGER in preparing catalog cards for books and periodicals. Assigns classification numbers, descriptive headings, and explanatory summaries to book and catalog cards to facilitate locating and obtaining materials. Composes annotations (explanatory summaries) of material content.

EDUCATIONAL AND TRAINING REQUIREMENTS
Master's degree in Library Science. Training time from 1 to 4 years, depending on areas of responsibility, and size and complexity of library system.

COLLECTOR, OVERDUE MATERIAL
1-15.69
(240.368)

OCCUPATIONAL DEFINITION
	Collects fines and overdue library material from borrowers: Sorts copies of overdue notices, according to street addresses, to plan collection route. Drives to address shown on overdue notice and explains purpose of call to borrower. Attempts to obtain overdue material and fine, or library card. Collects payment for lost material. Schedules return appointment to obtain material not on premises or advises borrower of alternative methods of returning materials. Records reasons for failure to collect material on overdue notice.

EDUCATIONAL AND TRAINING REQUIREMENTS
High school graduate. Training time, one week.

FIELD LIBRARIAN
0-23.01
(100.118)
library consultant; state field consultant

OCCUPATIONAL DEFINITION
	Advises administrators, members of trustee boards, and civic groups on matters designed to improve the organization, administration, and service of public libraries: Discusses personnel staffing patterns, building plans, and book collections with

administrators who request consultation service from State. Analyzes administrative policies, observes work procedures, and reviews data relative to book collections to determine effectiveness of library service to public. Compares allotments designated for building funds, salaries, and book collections with standards prepared by State agencies, to determine effectiveness of budget. Gathers statistical data, such as population and community growth rates, and analyzes building plans to determine adequacy of programs for expansion. Prepares evaluation of library systems based on observations and surveys, and recommends measures to improve organization and administration of systems according to state program for libraries and professional experience. Presents surveys of salary standards, budget analyses, and tentative building programs to administrators as suggested means of improving administration of library systems. Negotiates with civic groups, boards of trustees and library administrators who wish to consolidate library systems to resolve jurisdictional disputes and differences of opinion. Informs citizen groups of state legal requirements relative to library consolidations. Explains eligibility requirements for programs offering State and Federal financial assistance to libraries and recommends measures to be taken to attain eligibility and apply for aid. Plans and organizes programs for the recruitment of professional personnel. Directs the establishment of work procedures in new or reorganized library systems. Recommends methods of enlarging book collections. Plans and organizes training programs for administrators to inform them of recent developments in public administration and library science. Addresses town meetings and civic organizations to explain programs offered by State Division of Libraries. Occasionally demonstrates or performs all professional and clerical tasks associated with public libraries.

EDUCATIONAL AND TRAINING REQUIREMENTS
Master's degree in Library Science. Approximately five years of experience in professional library work, with at least two years as administrator.

FILM LIBRARIAN
0-23.10
(100.168)
audiovisual librarian; film-and-record librarian

OCCUPATIONAL DEFINITION
Plans film programs and keeps library of film and other audio-visual materials: Reviews records/CDs and motion-picture soundtracks, and motion pictures, considering their technical, informational, and esthetic qualities, to select materials for library collection. Prepares brief summary of film content for catalog. Prepares and arranges film programs for presentation to groups. Advises those planning to install film program on technical problems, such as acoustics, lighting, and program content, and leads discussions after film showing. May maintain or oversee maintenance of audio and video material. Operates audio/video equipment, film projectors, CD/DVD players, splicers, rewinders, and film-inspection equipment.

EDUCATIONAL AND TRAINING REQUIREMENTS
Master's degree in Library Science with additional training in film production techniques.

LIBRARIAN
0-23.20
(100.168)

OCCUPATIONAL DEFINITION

Selects and maintains library collection of books, periodicals, documents, films, recordings, media technology and other materials, and assists groups and individuals to locate and obtain materials: Furnishes information on library activities, facilities, rules, and services. Explains use of reference sources, such as bibliographic indexes, reading guides, the Internet and online applications to locate information. Describes or demonstrates procedures for searching catalog files, shelf collections and online and media applications to obtain materials. Searches catalog files and shelves to locate information. Issues and receives materials for circulation or for use in library. Assembles and arranges displays of books and other library materials. Performs variety of duties to maintain reference and circulation matter, such as copying author's name and title on catalog cards, and selecting and assembling pictures and newspaper clippings. Answers correspondence on special reference subjects. May compile book titles, bibliographies, or reading lists according to subject matter or designated interests to prepare reading lists. May select, order, catalog and classify materials. Librarians also compile lists of books, periodicals, articles, and audio-visual materials on particular subjects; analyze collections; and recommend materials. They collect and organize books, pamphlets, manuscripts, and other materials in a specific field, such as rare books, genealogy, or music. In addition, they coordinate programs such as storytelling for children and literacy skills and book talks for adults, conduct classes, publicize services, provide reference help, write grants, and oversee other administrative matters. When engaged in locating information on specific subjects is known as Reference Librarian.

EDUCATIONAL AND TRAINING REQUIREMENTS

Master's degree in Library Science. Training time of six months to two years, depending on nature of assignment.

LIBRARIAN, SPECIAL COLLECTIONS
0-23.10
(100.168)

OCCUPATIONAL DEFINITION

Collects books, pamphlets, manuscripts, and rare newspapers, to provide source material for research: Organizes collections according to field of interest. Examines reference works and consults specialists preparatory to selecting materials for collections. Compiles bibliographies. Appraises subject materials, using references, such as bibliographies, book auction records, and special catalogs. Publishes papers and bibliographies on special collections to notify clientele of available materials. Lectures on booklore, such as history of printing, bindings, and illuminations. May plan and arrange displays for library exhibits. May index and reproduce materials for sale to other libraries. May specialize in rare books and be known as Rare Book Librarian.

EDUCATIONAL AND TRAINING REQUIREMENTS
Master's degree in Library Science. Training time may range up to five years, depending on complexity of field and size of collection.

LIBRARIAN, SPECIAL LIBRARY
0-23.20
(100.118)

OCCUPATIONAL DEFINITION
Manages library or section containing specialized materials for industrial, commercial, or governmental organizations, or for such institutions as schools and hospitals: Arranges special collections of technical books, periodicals, manufacturers' catalogs and specifications, film strips, motion pictures, CD/DVD and other media, and journal reprints. Searches literature, compiles accession lists, and annotates or abstracts materials. Assists patrons in research problems. May translate or order translation of materials from foreign languages into English. May be designated according to subject matter or specialty of library or department as Art Librarian; Business Librarian; Engineering Librarian; Law Librarian; Map Librarian; Medical Librarian.

EDUCATIONAL AND TRAINING REQUIREMENTS
Master's degree in Library Science. Training time, 1 to 2 years.

LIBRARY ASSISTANT
1-20.01
(100.368)
book loan clerk; circulation clerk; desk attendant;
library aid; library attendant; library clerk; library helper

OCCUPATIONAL DEFINITION
Compiles records, sorts and shelves books, and issues and receives library materials, such as books, films, and CD-ROM: Records identifying data and due date on cards by hand or using photographic equipment to issue books to patrons. Inspects returned books for damage, verifies due date, and computes and receives overdue fines. Reviews records to compile list of overdue books and issues overdue notices to borrowers. Sorts books, publications, and other items according to classification code and returns them to shelves, files, or other designated storage area. Locates books and publications for patrons. Issues borrower's identification card according to established procedures. Files cards in catalog drawers according to system. Repairs books. Answers inquiries of nonprofessional nature on telephone and in person and refers persons requiring professional assistance to LIBRARIAN. May type material cards or issue cards and duty schedules. May be designated according to type of library as Bookmobile Clerk; Branch-Library Clerk; according to assigned department as Library Clerk, Art Department; or may be known according to tasks performed as Library Clerk, Book Return.

EDUCATIONAL AND TRAINING REQUIREMENTS
High school graduate. Training time, 6 to 12 months.

LIBRARY ASSOCIATE DIRECTOR
0-23.01
(100.118)
assistant director, library; associated librarian; deputy librarian

OCCUPATIONAL DEFINITION
Directs and assists with formulation and administration of library policies and procedures: Confers with department heads to coordinate reference services with technical processing and circulation activities. Meets with subordinate supervisory personnel to discuss goals and problems in library system. Observes functions in branch libraries to insure that established policies and work procedures are followed. Confers with LIBRARY DIRECTOR to discuss methods for increasing the efficiency of library service. Recommends reclassification of library jobs based on specific criteria of job evaluation, such as complexity of duties and scope of responsibility. Visits colleges, universities, and professional organizations to recruit workers. Forecasts growth of community from analysis of statistical data and plans building programs and expansion of library service into new areas. Acts for LIBRARY DIRECTOR in his absence.

EDUCATIONAL AND TRAINING REQUIREMENTS
Master's degree in Library Science. Training time approximately 4 to 6 years, serving in various professional and supervisory positions in a library system.

LIBRARY DIRECTOR
0-23.01
(100.118)
librarian, head; library administrator; library superintendent; manager, library

OCCUPATIONAL DEFINITION
Plans and administers program of library services: Submits recommendations on library policies and services to governing body, such as board of directors or board of trustees, and implements policy decisions. Analyzes, selects, and executes recommendations of subordinates, such as department chiefs or branch supervisors. Analyzes and coordinates departmental budget estimates and controls expenditures to administer approved budget. Reviews and evaluates orders for books, films, and advanced media, examines trade publications and samples, interviews publishers' representatives, and consults with subordinates to select materials. Administers personnel regulations, interviews and appoints job applicants, rates staff performance, and promotes and discharges employees. Plans and conducts staff meetings and participates in community and professional committee meetings to discuss library problems. Delivers book reviews and lectures to publicize library activities and services. May examine and select materials to be discarded, repaired, or replaced. May be designated according to governmental subdivision served as City-Library Director; County-Library Director.

EDUCATIONAL AND TRAINING REQUIREMENTS
Master's degree in Library Science. Training time approximately 4 to 8 years, serving in various professional and supervisory positions in a library system.

PAGE
1-23.14
(109.687)
library page; runner; shelver; shelving clerk; stack clerk

OCCUPATIONAL DEFINITION
Locates library materials such as books, periodicals, and pictures for loan, and replaces material in shelving area (stacks) or files, according to identification number and title. Trucks or carries material between shelving area and issue desk. May cut premarked articles from periodicals.

EDUCATIONAL AND TRAINING REQUIREMENTS
Tenth to twelfth grade. Training time from 1 to 3 months.

PATIENTS' LIBRARIAN
0-23.20
(100.168)
hospital librarian

OCCUPATIONAL DEFINITION
Analyzes reading needs of patients and provides library services for patients and employees in hospital or similar institution: Furnishes readers' advisory services on basis of knowledge of current reviews and bibliographies. Reviews requests, and selects books and other library materials for ward trips according to mental state, educational background, and special needs of patients. Writes book reviews for hospital bulletins or newspapers and circulates reviews among patients. Provides handicapped or bedridden patients with reading aids, such as prism glasses, page turners, book stands, or talking books, and with other audio-visual material and aids. (This job is a specialization of LIBRARIAN and shares the same basic duties. See LIBRARIAN.)

EDUCATIONAL AND TRAINING REQUIREMENTS
Master's degree in Library Science. Training time, six months.

REGISTRATION CLERK
1-20.01
(109.368)

OCCUPATIONAL DEFINITION
Registers library patrons to permit them to borrow books, periodicals, and other library materials: Copies identifying data, such as name and address, from application onto registration list and borrowers' cards to register borrowers, and issues cards to

borrowers. Records changes of address or name onto registration list and borrowers' cards to amend records.

EDUCATIONAL AND TRAINING REQUIREMENTS
High school graduate. Training time, 6 to 12 months.

SCHOOL LIBRARIAN
0-23.20
(100.168)

OCCUPATIONAL DEFINITION
Provides library service which includes book and audio-visual material selection, circulation, promotional work, reference, and general administration: Serves as a resource specialist for teachers, counselors, and other faculty members. Guides students in their reading and in use of communication media. (This job is a specialization of LIBRARIAN and shares the same basic duties. See LIBRARIAN.)

EDUCATIONAL AND TRAINING REQUIREMENTS
Master's degree in Library Science. Training time of 6 months to 2 years.

SHELVING SUPERVISOR
1-20.01
(109.138)
stack supervisor

OCCUPATIONAL DEFINITION
Supervises and coordinates activities of library workers engaged in replacing books and other materials on shelves according to library classification system: Assigns duties to workers. Trains and directs workers in performance of shelving tasks. Examines materials on shelves to verify accuracy of placement. Counts number of materials placed on shelves to record shelving activity. Marks designated classification number, subject matter, or title, to arrange material for shelving.

EDUCATIONAL AND TRAINING REQUIREMENTS
High school graduate. Training time, one year.

YOUNG ADULT LIBRARIAN
0-23.10
(100.288)

OCCUPATIONAL DEFINITION
Directs young adult program in library to provide special activities for high school and college-age readers: Organizes young adults activities, such as chess clubs, creative writing club, and photography contests. Contacts speakers, writes and distributes advertising, and meets young adult club representatives to prepare group programs. Delivers talks on books to stimulate reading. Addresses groups such as

parent-teacher associations and civic organizations, to inform community of activities. Conducts high school classes on Library Tours to acquaint students with library facilities and services. Compiles lists of young adult reading materials for individuals, high school classes, and branch libraries. Issues and receives library materials, such as books and phonograph records. (This job is a specialization of LIBRARIAN and shares the same basic duties. See LIBRARIAN.)

EDUCATIONAL AND TRAINING REQUIREMENTS
Master's degree in Library Science with an additional one year training time.

ANSWER SHEET

TEST NO. _____ PART _____ TITLE OF POSITION _____
(AS GIVEN IN EXAMINATION ANNOUNCEMENT - INCLUDE OPTION, IF ANY)

PLACE OF EXAMINATION _____ (CITY OR TOWN) _____ (STATE) _____ DATE _____

RATING

USE THE SPECIAL PENCIL. MAKE GLOSSY BLACK MARKS.

Make only ONE mark for each answer. Additional and stray marks may be counted as mistakes. In making corrections, erase errors COMPLETELY.

SAYVILLE LIBRARY
88 GREENE AVENUE
SAYVILLE, NY 11782

ANSWER SHEET

JUL 2 0 2009

TEST NO. _____ PART _____ TITLE OF POSITION _____

(AS GIVEN IN EXAMINATION ANNOUNCEMENT - INCLUDE OPTION, IF ANY)

PLACE OF EXAMINATION _____   DATE _____

(CITY OR TOWN)   (STATE)

RATING

USE THE SPECIAL PENCIL. MAKE GLOSSY BLACK MARKS.

Make only ONE mark for each answer. Additional and stray marks may be counted as mistakes. In making corrections, erase errors COMPLETELY.